Polemics and Provocations

Polemics and Provocations

Essays in Anticipation of the Daughter

PAUL GILK

WIPF & STOCK · Eugene, Oregon

POLEMICS AND PROVOCATIONS
Essays in Anticipation of the Daughter

Wipf & Stock
An Imprint of Wipf and Stock Publishers
199 W. 8th Ave., Suite 3
Eugene, OR 97401

www.wipfandstock.com

ISBN 13: 978-1-60899-371-0

Manufactured in the U.S.A.

For my daughter Hannah

To believe that a later point in time necessarily carries a larger accumulation of values, or that the latest invention necessarily brings a human improvement, is to forget the patent evidence of history: the recurrent lapses into barbarism, most conspicuous, and most dreadful, as Giambattista Vico long ago pointed out, in the behavior of *civilized* man. Was the Inquisition, with its ingenious mechanical innovations in nicely graded torture, a sign of progress? Technically, Yes: humanly, No. From the standpoint of human survival, to say nothing of further development, a flint arrowhead is preferable to a hydrogen bomb. Doubtless it hurts the pride of modern man to realize that earlier cultures, with simpler technical facilities, may have been superior to his own in terms of human values, and that genuine progress involves continuity and conservation, above all, conscious anticipation and rational selection—the antithesis of our present kaleidoscopic multiplication of random novelties.

Lewis Mumford,
"Progress as 'Science Fiction,'" in *The Pentagon of Power*, pages 203–4

For [Rene] Girard, what is happening to us is the paradoxical effect of the underground workings of the gospel message, a message which, when it is only partially understood—when people have yet to radically abandon their violence—produces more, not less, violence, but a violence increasingly contained and increasingly deferred. The message acts like a ruse: this growing and ever-postponed violence is leading us to a point of bifurcation in which our responsibility will be total: either the inauguration of the Kingdom of Love or else a destructive apocalypse for which we will have only ourselves to blame.

Jean-Pierre Dupuy,
"Detour and Sacrifice," in *The Challenges of Ivan Illich*, page 202

The world of our time is in confusion. It is reaching the peak of the greatest crisis in history. Never before has there been such a total upheaval of the whole human race. Tremendous forces are at work, spiritual, sociological, economic, technological and . . . political. Mankind stands on the brink of a new barbarism, yet at the same time there remain possibilities for an unexpected and almost unbelievable solution, the creation of a new world and a new civilization the like of which has never been seen. We are face to face either with Antichrist or the Millennium, no one knows which.

Thomas Merton,
"Epilogue," in *The Silent Life*, pages 151–52

But it is well to understand the simple truth that western civilization has always defined itself in opposition to nature—as Freud said, civilization was necessary "to defend us from nature," including our own—and to realize that this opposition is crucial to the way the civilization views itself and operates.

Kirkpatrick Sale,
"The Erectus Alternative," in *After Eden*, page 127

[T]he dialectic of sublimation in civilization is cumulative, cumulatively abstract and cumulatively deadening . . . .

Norman O. Brown,
"Apollo and Dionysus," in *Life Against Death: The Psycholanalytical Meaning of History*, page 173

Perhaps this is the issue that frightens the prophets. A people may be dying without being aware of it; a people may be able to survive, yet refuse to make use of their ability.

Abraham J. Heschel,
"Introduction," in *The Prophets*, page xii

Contents

Contents

Acknowledgments

As a reclusive writer with no computer, internet, or marketing competence, I am vulnerable to emotional meltdown when persons appear who not only get what I've been trying to say, but who also express a sincere and energetic desire to infect others with their enthusiasm. When *Green Politics Is Eutopian* came out, Bill Hurrle and Nick Vander Puy were such persons. They arrived at the log house with venison, wild rice, and—for Bill—an undiagnosed cancer of the esophagus that brought him to his death in less than eight months. It's a little late to say Thank You, but, as my Mama used to insist, Better late than never.

Once again there would be no finished book were it not for my dear friend Carol Ann Okite. Her kindness, competence, patience, and commitment have kept my writing projects moving. I don't know that I deserve such wonderful collaboration, but I am deeply grateful for it.

And, finally, I want to acknowledge the passing of Howard Zinn, who taught us all to look at history from the bottom up.

Introduction

THESE ESSAYS BEGAN IN January 2007 almost as pure writing exercises, if I might risk use of the word "pure." And, since it was close to Lent (and then into it), I originally thought of the essays as being "for Lent." It was a handy tag, but not one that stuck. To some extent, I was experimenting with sermon-length pieces of writing, although for what purpose was completely unclear, since I had no access to a pulpit. One piece of writing led to another until, over the course of a year, more or less, there appeared, to my astonishment, another book-length manuscript.

When my ninety-five year-old father nearly died of an apparent stroke in December of 2007, I dealt with my distress and anxiety by having a belated argument with him about religious matters. It was an argument only on paper, and totally one-sided. "An Unseemly Eulogy for My Father" therefore concludes these essays/sermons/polemics in a way that makes the overall argument more personal and, perhaps, more grounded.

However, my wife Susanna tells me these growly sermonettes are little more than repetitive hissy fits. Perhaps that's so. (I think, no doubt immodestly, of the painter Camille Pissarro and his seemingly endless landscapes.) I therefore offer the following poem, written in the early 1970s, as an appropriate way to establish the mood.

THE PAMPHLETEER POET

The pamphleteer poet
          comes riding
his pony-express nag,
            sway-backed,
    heavy-footed,
        in a cloud of acrid dust,
  bringing news
          of questionable importance
in his thick-skinned
        grimy satchel,
smelling
      of repetitious
          sweats.

In the Image of God

A s we all know, there has been (and will continue to be) a lot of talk about Islam, the relationship between Islam, Christianity, and Judaism, and about all three religions as "Abrahamic." These religions are composed of monotheists who as People of the Book should have, in principle, more to share and agree on than to squabble over or fight about. And so the bulk of conversation, at least on the liberal or Left side of the political and religious spectrum, congeals in the direction of tolerance, dialogue, and friendly exchange, stressing the importance of learning to understand one another through courteous listening and perhaps even liturgical sharing.

I ambiguously concur with this impulse, this point of view. At its deepest level, such a stance is not merely humane but also embodies, when push comes to shove, or when harsh rhetoric translates into bullets and bombs, the Gospel directive to help the stranger and love the enemy. I say this now for two reasons. First, I believe the Gospel directive is true. That is, I believe helping the stranger and loving the enemy leads to or at least points toward that place we might call the kingdom of God, invoking by that term the primary concept utilized by Jesus in the first three Gospels. But the second reason I mention the directive to help the stranger and love the enemy is that, for all the inflated "Christian" posturing in this country, with all the righteous self-assertion and self-promotion of ourselves as a "Christian" nation, our method of expressing this Christian nationhood toward the rest of the world comes largely in the form of battle groups, aircraft carriers, attack aircraft, drones, bombs, missiles, guns, soldiers, sailors, airmen, and marines. We "love" our enemies with the sword. We may wish to see our enemies "saved," but first we have to vigorously suppress their false convictions and bad attitudes. This may be

a righteous expression of so-called Tough Love, but it is a dreadful corruption of the Gospels.

So while I truly believe Jesus was and is right in his prescription of
radical servanthood and radical stewardship, I also believe that Christianity
has, for the most part, weaseled out of this hard, simple requirement by
creating for itself a truly elegant rationalization and complex justification
for righteous imperialism.[1] Furthermore (though some may say I am on
shakier ground), I generalize from the Christian situation to the Islamic
and Jewish situations by saying I suspect there may be as few Moslems or
as few Jews, proportionately, who have immolated their egos in the fire of
the divine as there are Christians who have done so. Righteousness may
ignite the ego to halogen-bulb brightness, while humility is content with
the flickering illumination of candlelight. Righteousness is the brilliant
radiance of blind arrogance mixed with unexamined presumption.

In other words, I believe that religions are largely cultural constructs
catering to what seems to be a universal human craving for alignment
with cosmic authority and moral self-justification. We seem to want to
believe that the group I belong to knows the Truth, and I am therefore
under the moral umbrella of that Truth. Therefore I am a good and (if you
really want to know) a superior person by virtue of my religious affiliation. I doubt if there is need here to expound on such concepts as Chosen
People, Manifest Destiny, Holy War, or American Exceptionalism.

II

I say all this as prelude. That is, for all our talk of dialogue and tolerance, as
important as these concepts and practices may be, we are living in fantasy
if we think dialogue and tolerance are about to rule human behavior any
time soon. We may earnestly desire dialogue and tolerance, we may strive
for those spiritual qualities and pray until sweat rolls down our faces (I
am not making fun, although I am suggesting our passion is rather tepid),
but we are not only to be as innocent as doves but also as wise as serpents.
Plus it is perfectly reasonable to say that *real* dialogue and *real* tolerance
depend on *real* soul-searching and *real* repentance, and that means facing
into and coming to grips with how fully our inherited sense of superiority serves to justify our comfortable array of empire privileges in a spiri-

---

1. For a thorough examination of how Christianity relates to war, see W. Michael
Slattery's *Jesus the Warrior?*

tual as well as a material sense. You may therefore take (and perhaps you should take) what I am about to say as serpent's wisdom, or maybe just forked-tongued gibberish. I am going to share with you the insight, vision, revelation, or serpent's hallucination that came to me almost exactly thirty years ago and that, if anything, has strengthened over the subsequent three decades.

But first I need to sketch a preamble to the serpent's bite.

III

I grew up on a small farm in northern Wisconsin, perhaps one of the last "Jeffersonian" enclaves of small-scale farm culture in the country. And when, as a young man in St. Louis, I missed that rural life, that agrarian culture, even as I was aware small farms were dying, I asked smart people to explain to me *why* small farms were dying. The answers I received were unsatisfactory at best, so I began to study the history of agriculture in a catch-as-catch-can sort of way. I read a lot. But to drop only two names here, I was greatly influenced by the great American historian Lewis Mumford and by that classics professor turned explicator of Freud, Norman O. Brown.

More or less simultaneously with this agrarian preoccupation, there were at least two additional preoccupations eating at me. One, thanks to the seemingly endless American war to demolish Vietnam (Daniel Ellsberg, in his *Secrets*, traces American intrusion back to the Truman administration), was the prevalence of aggressive, brutal militarism in the history of civilization. Why was war so common, especially at the level of civilized empire? Another preoccupation, thanks to the rise of the women's movement, was whether feminism had a deeper meaning than mere idiosyncratic social corrective, whether it represented something greater than minor reform. That is, do women merely want in on the game of empire, or do they want to fundamentally restructure the game itself in the direction of equality and conservation?

These elements—the origins of agriculture in the gathering activities of Neolithic women, the impoundment of the agrarian village and its economic abundance by male warriors at the dawn of civilization, the inherently militaristic and imperial nature of warrior civilization, and the modern rise of feminist rebellion—began to cook and bubble inside me, along with a growing awareness of global ecological devastation. Here I need to invoke two additional steps that led to my serpent's revelation.

3

IV

First, I learned in reading about Karl Marx and Friedrich Engels that the profemale anthropology that Engels in particular brought to the table of political agitation had come from a book called *Mother Right*, an early work of archeology by a Swiss scholar named Johann Jakob Bachofen. In his book, Bachofen insisted, on the basis of his scholarly findings, that underlying patriarchal civilization was a matriarchal stratum, represented by all manner of goddesses in statuary form. He called this stratum *Mutterreich* or Mother Rule. Second, from reading Michael Harrington's *Socialism*, in an early chapter where Harrington surveys what he considered the Western antecedents of socialist values, I learned about a twelfth-century Italian monk, a Cistercian named Joachim of Floris (or Fiore), who created a conceptual schema, based on a meshing of the Christian Trinity with the Old and New Testaments, positing Three Ages in human history: the Age of the Father, characterized by monarchy, discipline, and law; the Age of the Son, characterized as love institutionalized in the church; and, still to come, an Age of the Holy Ghost, characterized as consecrated (or holy) anarchy.[II]

It apparently took a while for the Church of Rome to realize it didn't like this schema, for it implied the obsolescence of the church's rule and the disintegration of its supremacy in Western Europe. But that realization was slow enough in coming so that Joachim got to die a natural death. Some of his followers may not have been so fortunate.

When the serpent of wisdom bit, it was with both fangs. One fang was named Bachofen. The other was named Joachim. The intoxicating wisdom injected through those fangs entered a reservoir full of unresolved cultural turmoil in which Mumford and Brown, feminism and civilized militarism, the impoundment of Neolithic agrarian abundance and contemporary ecological limitation were all interacting in a bubbling pool ready and even eager for spiritual liberation. When the serpent bit and the intoxicants struck home, this was the ensuing revelation: there are not Three Ages to think about; there are *Four*. It was not just Father, Son, and Holy Ghost, but *Mother*, Father, Son, and Holy Ghost.

II. Tony Allan, in his *Prophecies*, page 32, describes the Father's age as "an epoch of law, obedience, hierarchy, fear and servitude," the Son's age as "an era of grace, faith and filial submission," and the Holy Spirit's age as "an epoch of love, freedom, contemplation, community and joy."

But wait! Something there did not quite ring true. Some feminist theologians were insisting the Holy Ghost (or Holy Spirit) was and is feminine. And so the configuration was not just Mother, Father, Son, and Holy Ghost, but, to be psychologically consistent, it had to be Mother, Father, Son, and *Daughter. That* was the insight, the revelation that forever changed my life.

V

I wish to bring this back to the beginning, back to the three Abrahamic religions and to why I believe tolerance and humane dialogue are not going to rule the newspaper headlines any time soon. The three Abrahamic religions, in their orthodox, conventional expressions, can certainly be seen as determined and even fierce repositories of male presumption, mythic cores of male prerogative. The divine when identified as strictly Father, God when perceived as exclusively Male, generates religions that elevate maleness into psychological, cultural, and spiritual superiority.[III] Looked at psychoanalytically—here I take a deep bow to Norman O. Brown—religions with explicit and exclusive male divinity arose as a consequence of the victorious warrior energy at the heart of Middle Eastern civilization. Without warrior civilization, the three Abrahamic religions, with their exclusively male divinity, are simply unthinkable.

Civilization congealed precisely at that point where, by armed force and political coercion, male warriors expropriated the agricultural abundance of the precivilized agrarian village, and this abundance was overwhelmingly the product of a feminine horticulture that had its origin in the attentive experimentation of female gatherers. The divinity of this village abundance was the Mother. Warrior civilization crushed Her. This is what Johann Jakob Bachofen discovered and taught.

In terms of historical stages, Mother, Father, and Son clearly work. It's possible to lay such a schema on actual historical progression. The question is whether Daughter is spiritually prophetic or merely New Age

---

III. Elaine Pagels, in the opening sentences of chapter 3 ("God the Father/God the Mother") in *The Gnostic Gospels*, page 48, says "Unlike many of his contemporaries among the deities of the ancient Near East, the God of Israel shared his power with no female divinity, nor was he the divine Husband or Lover of any. He can scarcely be characterized in any but masculine epithets: king, lord, master, judge, and father. Indeed, the absence of feminine symbolism for God marks Judaism, Christianity, and Islam in striking contrast to the world's other religious traditions. . . ."

fluff. In proposing such a modification of Joachim's vision I am, no doubt, also incriminating myself as a Christian heretic. I am bending or expanding the Christian Trinity into a post-Christian Mandala. I am saying that if the divine can be imputed to have gender, if we are made in the image of a gendered divine, then the divine is as much Female as it is Male. If there is a Father, there has to be a Mother. If there's a Son, there has to be a Daughter. Either no gender or both genders. God as strictly Male is idolatrous.

VI

Now—I will compact these final remarks mercilessly, as befits a person under the influence of serpent hallucinogens—the coercive globalization of civilization, as a system of imperial male conquest and violent righteousness, has brought us to a Global Crisis, as the newspapers so wisely and regularly inform us. This crisis is political, it is economic, it is cultural, it is ecological, and it is religious. It is in the gendered imagery of the divine—an imagery we psychologically internalize—where an immeasurably large portion of our contemporary global crisis is lodged. The underlying force of globalization in its dominant mode is male warrior energy, simultaneously aggressive and righteous. This energy has both shaped and infected all Abrahamic religions, regarding themselves as superior, chosen, and virtuous above all others. This energy claims divine legitimacy. It has contempt for the troubling self-critical and certainly for the feminine. It conflates male presumption with the will of God. It therefore acts with the arrogance of holy entitlement and, when obstructed or opposed, it acts or can act with righteous sadism.

The Four Ages of the divine—Mother, Father, Son, and Daughter—implies that the Age of the Son will be superseded by the Age of the Daughter, an age of "consecrated anarchy," as Joachim (or Michael Harrington) so giddily put it. If so, how do we get there? Let's start by acknowledging that the women's movement, broadly speaking, is alive and well, even if its energy has gone largely into an integration with what previously have been overwhelmingly male domains—law, medicine, business, and the clergy. For the last forty or fifty years, women have been flooding the basement of the male Establishment, and the female water level keeps rising. The Global Crisis, however, is alive and increasingly unwell, and its unwellness grows with every passing month and year. The magnitude of crisis is compounding, with Climate Change and Population Growth closing in by leaps and bounds. The handwriting is not only on the wall, it is flashing off and on with manic urgency.

At the heart of this accelerating crisis is civilized male arrogance with its sense of cosmic entitlement. The driving engine of global breakdown is the blind, arrogant, aggressive, unrelenting industrial and financial globalization of male-controlled civilization. And in the jaws of Global Crisis the options become quite stark. One option is annihilation, some variation of End Times, disaster minus rapture, disaster minus any divine rescue, just unremitting desolation. Another option (an unlikely one) is sudden enlightenment or repentance on a scale broad enough to cause global transformation of spiritual and political consciousness. Another option is the restoration, on a more or less global scale, of multiethnic aristocracy living in great affluence while the rest of us grub the best we can under their humorless surveillance and vicious SWAT teams. Another option (as the Cradle of Civilization re-emerges as its Coffin) is blind male entitlement corralling itself in a cul-de-sac of unremitting violence, a cul-de-sac in which the three Abrahamic religions smash and smash and smash each other to the point where two things happen: male exhaustion and economic breakdown on the one hand, and, on the other, female outrage of such depth and intensity that, surpassing all the customary conventions of polite gender deference, women simply thrust men aside and take things over.

I would very much prefer the unlikely second option—repentance, enlightenment, and voluntary transformation. But I see that people (even those who know better) are so locked into their conventional mental boxes that I am steadily losing whatever hope I may once have had for sufficient, significant, large-scale voluntary change. Our inertia and immobility help to build energy toward violence and breakdown, and our passivity, even as mere consumers of global commodities, feeds the violence and increases the likelihood of breakdown.

Practically speaking, the restoration of aristocracy would seem to have the greatest chance of success, given that the history of civilization is almost entirely based on elite, aristocratic control. Wealth is already so congealed in the top one percent of the population that aristocratic restoration is no fanciful stretch.[IV] But I am left pondering this formulation—

IV. Oswald Spengler in the abridged version of *The Decline of the West*, pages 361 and 362, says "the true class-State is an expression of the general historical experience that it

7

Mother, Father, Son, and Daughter—and I believe we are in for a really big surprise. What we might call the Second Coming of Christ is about to occur; only the Christ that's coming is dressed in a female body. I am praying for her speedy arrival, and I urge you to do so, too. Thank you very much for your impatience.

---

is always a single social stratum which, constitutionally or otherwise, provides the political leading. It is always a definite minority that represents the world-historical tendency of a State . . . , a closed circle of persons possessing homogeneous practical gifts, which constantly recruits itself and preserves in its midst the whole sum of unwritten political tradition and experience." In other words, an inevitable aristocratic restoration.

2

Temper Tantrum

I N THE PREVIOUS ESSAY, I posited a conceptual framework of Four Ages—Mother, Father, Son, and Daughter—and, in passing, said the great bulk of civilized history is the history of aristocratic control. I implied, but did not explicitly say, that our grasp and practice of democracy is therefore weak and, in the not-too-distant future, the restoration of an explicit aristocracy could be a very real possibility. I now make those assertions explicit—that our psychological grasp and historical practice of democracy is functionally weak, and that aristocracy is steadily building its bulwark of wealth and power behind veiled corporate compounds—and it is that fact (or at least that assertion) I wish to explore.

First I want to say that almost all of us, rather reflexively, are happy to say we are civilized. Even more than happy, we can be rather insistent on the point. More important than being democrats (with a small d), we give ethical priority to being under the moral umbrella of civility and the political shield of civilization. First civilization then democracy, if we were to put our ruling concepts in proper order. We seem to believe that only civilized people can be truly democratic. But, since we believe we already function as a democratic society, our thinking about these concepts, these categories of civilization and democracy, does not cause us many sleepless nights. We are pretty much at peace with our democratic civility. We may fret that the executive branch of government may have more autonomy in relation to congress than we would like or that money plays far too big a role in elections. But we see these as constitutional dilemmas the courts (or constitutional amendments) will resolve rather than as deeper historical and even religious problems that may involve the inadequacies of our two-party system or flaws within the Constitution itself. The cultural ramifications of our understanding of democracy are dependent on the ethical content of our spirituality, in other words. How we view our responsibility toward our global neighbors is also, at its deepest, lodged in our religious convictions.

Yet the world is rapidly going to hell in a handbasket: enough nuclear weapons on hair-trigger alert to wipe out most higher life forms on Earth, lots of armed conflicts around the world (many of which have an American coloration, certainly including the dreadful and disastrous wars in Afghanistan and Iraq), consumption of Earth's resources far beyond ecological sustainability, a Global Warming driving Earth's atmosphere and oceans into an unpredictably calamitous Climate Change, and any number of other woes, including a rapidly widening wealth chasm globally between rich and poor.[I]

My thesis is that civilization from its inception, roughly five thousand years ago, has been inherently and explicitly antidemocratic and antiecological. Insofar as the precivilized agrarian village in some ways was democratic, civilization rose to dominance by overpowering folk control of the agrarian subsistence economy and its village self-governance. Folk evolution was thereafter thwarted and constrained. Civilization was invariably based on militarism and exploitation, and this required the economic impoundment of the folk community. Civilization always generated an aristocracy, and that aristocracy was simultaneously an economic and political elite.[II] The "democratization" of civilization, in spite of

I. Kirkpatrick Sale, in his 2006 book *After Eden*, asks us (on page 3) to "Consider the extent of our domination. Modern humans, now numbering six billion and predicted to go to ten billion, have left not one ecosystem on the surface of the earth free of pervasive human influence, transforming more than half the land on the planet for their own use (a quarter for farming and forestry, a quarter for pasture, 3 percent for industry, housing, and transport), consuming more than 40 percent of the total photosynthetic productivity of the sun, using 55 percent of the world's freshwater, controlling and regulating two-thirds of all the rivers and streams, and consuming a vast variety of plant, animal, and mineral resources, often to depletion, at a pace that is estimated not to be sustainable for more than fifty years." And Sale goes on to say that "It is this extraordinary dominance by one single bipedal species that has brought us to the present imperilment of the earth including the extinction of species, the destruction of ecosystems, the alteration of climate, the pollution of waters and soils, the exhaustion of fisheries, the elimination of forests, the spread of deserts, and the disruption of the atmosphere." The consequence "is that if western civilization continues its reckless policies and practices toward the earth we are headed toward *ecocide*." Or, as he sums up (on page 4): "our domination threatens our survival."

II. Oswald Spengler, in my abridged edition of *The Decline of the West*, page 245, says "Town and country differ in soul. . . . The peasant is eternal man, independent of all Cultures. The piety of the real peasant is older than Christianity, his gods older than limited modern advances in political democratic procedure, opened elite economic control to entrepreneurial opportunity. Every man a king, every home a castle. In a fairly short period of time, massive corporations have replaced aristocratic families as the primary holders of wealth and power. As sailing ships enabled European countries to engage in international commercial travel and military invasion (where was there one without the other?), the stage was being set for the economic conquering of the world, disguised, when and where necessary, as a missionary outreach program in behalf of civilization or Christianity, or both. Civilization globally supreme has brought us the woes Kirkpatrick Sale has itemized—Global Warming, etc.—but we cannot see the connection, we refuse to recognize the linkage, because to us civilization is a totally good, kind, uplifting, and benevolent concept. It is only a short step below God. It contains no evil. It casts no shadow. So we have an extremely difficult time even hearing that our comfortable self-concept as civilized democrats is the product of self-satisfied lazy thinking, the intellectual swaddling by which the affluent and the privileged wrap their eyes and ears so as not to see or hear about the real situation in the real world. Or, insofar as we recognize that the world is going to hell in a handbasket, it is certainly not our fault, not the fault of civilization, for we civilized people drive fuel-efficient cars and recycle our bottles and cans. If only everyone would be as civilized and not throw trash in alleys.

Nevertheless, I am asserting that our democracy is largely a sham, a cosmetic makeover of aristocratic presumptions, and representative of folk self-governance in only a fleeting and feeble sense. I could point to the percentage of wealth held by the top one percent in our society. I could point to the essential autonomy of the privately owned economy, most certainly including its corporate structure, as we elect people who are not at all inclined to bite the hand that feeds them or to propose serious democratic alterations either in how wealth is produced or in how it is distributed. (Consider the Wall Street debacle of October 2008, and the "too big to fail" federal bailout promoted by both the Bush and Obama administrations.) And as the industrial economy has evolved over the decades, it has obliterated much of the folk culture forms with

---

those of any of the higher religions. . . . What the house is to the peasant, a symbol of 'the settled,' the town is to the man of culture." In broad principle, Spengler is correct, except that the term to be associated with "the town" is not culture but civilization, and the "real" or "eternal" peasant may be better characterized as *woman* rather than *man*.

which it came in contact, from Native American tribal cultures to its own European-founded, subsistence agrarian villages to the "Jeffersonian" small-farm culture that was once so vigorous and wide-spread. In the place of previous cultural forms, most of which had enormous historical and cultural depth, the modern economy substituted novel commercial products and constraining civilized institutions. The folk past was explicitly deemed backward, primitive, and expendable. The past deserved to die. Civilization, via systematic industrialization, was finally able to begin to shed the cultural and spiritual drag of "backwardness." The civilized future could not be described with enough awe and adulation to possibly do it justice. Progress became our most important product, as Ronald Reagan told us when he sold refrigerators for General Electric. We would have electricity too cheap to meter from nuclear power plants. The utopia of civilized perfection was just around the corner. Glossy magazines and enthusiastic television programs gave us a glimpse into a technological heaven, at the turn of a page or the flip of a switch.[III]

This civilized, technological utopia is now in process of becoming a globalized, dystopian train wreck. The very elements within utopia, progress, and civilization that aggressively promised our sleepless liberation from torpid primitivity have revealed themselves to be agents of ecological and cultural disaster. So how, in the midst of all this, are we to understand the meaning of democracy? If what we presently have is democracy, and if this "democracy" is ecologically unsustainable and culturally disastrous, perhaps we would be wise to vote in a king, return ourselves to peasant servitude, and live—if not happily ever after—at least in a world of hugely reduced "democratic" consumption. We could return to envy of aristocratic opulence, and the world's ecology might begin to recover from the resource gangbang of "democratic" consumer rape.

It's possible we'll have an aristocratic restoration. Our collective spiritual encapsulation and cultural incompetence is so great that, by the time people begin to catch on that Halliburton and Blackwater are not reconstruction NGOs for broken democracies, it may be too late to pull the democratic fat out of the corporate/aristocratic fire. Fox News will have taken a predetermined "random" poll and democracy will have

III. In a full-page ad in *The Wall Street Journal* (page D4, September 24, 2009), the words "Alpha Never Sleeps" dominate the top half of the page. It is an ad for the "algorithmic and trading products" of Dow Jones & Co., Inc., and it expresses perfectly the manic hubris of civilized male self-obsession.

been "voted" obsolete. Rush Limbaugh and Glenn Beck will have been knighted. Sarah Palin will have been appointed President for Life.

Well, excuse the possible hyperbole, but we are confronted with three major options. The first option is disaster on such a scale that human population will be reduced to a tiny fraction of what it is today. The second is that powerful people with huge reserves of wealth will use episodic disasters, especially fear-provoking acts of terrorism, as political levers by which to re-establish explicit aristocracy. Of course, in the pauses between disasters, there will be lots of sincere ideological pleading for sharply reduced "entitlements," because, as we all know, the tax burden (especially on the rich) is an intolerable drag on the investment economy, especially in the context of an all-or-nothing global war on terror that we dare not fight with one hand tied behind our military's back. AM talk radio will keep the working class enlightened as to why "single-payer" healthcare and even Social Security are socialist traps needing to be militantly avoided and radically pruned.

The third option is a radical deepening of democratic consciousness. When Thoreau, in *Walden*, insists that villages should be universities, that what European noblemen, at their best, did for patronage of the arts, the democratic community as a whole should now do, we are in the terrain of such radically deepened consciousness. As Thoreau says, the "village should in some respects take the place of the nobleman of Europe. It should be the patron of the fine arts. It is rich enough. It wants only the magnanimity and refinement."[1]

But the truth is that we have very little of this deepened consciousness, as Thoreau repeatedly observed. We like to pretend we are brave sailors on the great blue sea of life, when all we have ever done is roll our pants legs and go wading to our ankles. We have been so coddled with the "patriotic" illusion that our Revolution in the late eighteenth century was so total, encompassing, vigorous, and profound, that all we have ever needed since was to enact the Emancipation Proclamation and women's suffrage. Our forefathers got it so fully right, so amazingly and comprehensively correct, that there's nothing for us to do but be strict constructionists and follow the letter of their nearly divine law. No wonder we believe in American Exceptionalism and Manifest Destiny as religious concepts. Our political and economic system is their literal embodiment. Our institutions are so close to perfect that the Pentagon is in the business of installing replicas of our near perfection around the world, especially where there is sufficient oil to lubricate the friction. We are so good, so fulfilled, and so fulfilling that it's hardly even possible to state the case in mere human terms. We are, as Madeleine Albright observed, the "indispensable nation."

Well, I have to say that I also know very little about this deepened democratic consciousness that we so badly need. I share fully in our collective ineptitude. But there are obvious lessons to be learned from our predicament. One lesson is that unlimited greed—or, to be more polite, unlimited appetite—is unsustainable and destructive. This is now a no-brainer. Global Warming and Peak Oil are about to bang our heads against this wall.[IV] Another lesson is that apocalyptic weaponry designed to protect strategic advantage would, if used, wipe out everybody's advantage and leave Earth a radioactive wasteland. And to believe it's all make-believe, that it couldn't, wouldn't, or won't happen, is to willfully believe in make-believe.

I find on reflection that I am *ashamed* of the human inheritance that aligns me with limitless appetite and insane selfish protectiveness. I am *ashamed* of my civilized presumptions. I find here fresh meaning for what *repentance* means; and so, by means of repentance, I begin to grasp that democracy must have a deep *spiritual* root, for what we must repent of is our privilege as protected by institutionalized violence and psychologically padded by ecclesiastical mythology. In the Christian tradition, Jesus' invocation of the "kingdom of God," as the social manifestation of radical servanthood and radical stewardship, is, for me, the fullest expression of the spiritual content of democratic self-governance. Democracy simply must be rooted in servanthood and stewardship to be viable. Earth may be able to tolerate aristocratic greed and selfishness, precisely because such rule is so assertively self-contained—its primary beneficiaries have belonged to a very restricted class—but Earth cannot tolerate "democratic" greed and selfishness because of the sheer magnitude of scale. If civilization for all means an aristocratic standard of living for everyone, then global ecology will become undone because of the destructively extractive polluting burden. Our current enlarging crisis proves that democracy must be governed by other drives than greed and fear or democracy itself will fail. Either deeper, more spiritual drives must come into play or there will be aristocratic regression or unmitigated devastation.

IV. For a detailed and extensive exploration into the "end" of oil—both its economic and its spiritual implications—see Maynard Kaufman's *Adapting to the End of Oil: Toward an Earth-Centered Spirituality.*

We need less the separation of church and state than a fusion of kingdom of God spirituality with democratic political aspiration. One finds, from Gandhi to Maslow, a psychology that teaches the maturation of spiritual self in proportion to the dissolvement of selfish ego.[V] And so we need—to put labels on it—libertarian, ecological, democratic socialism, a political metaphysics that has deepened beyond fear and greed into servanthood and stewardship. And we need this deepening very, very soon.

I say *libertarian* because liberty is a vital element within democratic self-governance. I say *ecological* because respect for the capacities and limitations of Creation is absolutely necessary for the stable conduct and self-restraint of democratic self-governance. And I say *socialism* for the following reasons. First, we all desire means by which we can maintain and, to some degree, participate in some sort of global engagement. Many of us have family or friends living thousands of miles away. We like to write to them, call them, visit them. We want to experience, if we can, crossing an ocean, walking in a desert or a tropical rain forest, being in an ancient city, moving in the midst of a culture totally different than our own. If the infrastructure that enables such engagement lies in private ownership, we are back to such concentration of wealth that ownership is already a nascent aristocracy. With nineteenth-century railroads we called such people "robber barons." Socialism enables a collective stewardship of concentrated wealth with *cooperative* responsibility.

In other words, a deeply democratic consciousness must be simultaneously libertarian, ecological, and socialist. And to those who dread centralist control, I say two things. First, what do you think we have now with a handful of unelected, undemocratic corporations providing us with our "consumer choices" or with two political parties that are, in the main, Empire and Empire Lite? Second, and more importantly, a fully articulated libertarian ecological democratic socialism would presuppose an enormous amount of decentralist folk initiative.[VI] An *ecological*

V. On pages 18 and 19 in the wonderful *Essays in Gandhian Economics*, in a rather lengthy Introduction by editors Romesh Diwan and Mark Lutz, there are even graphic representations of how the growth of spiritual Self implies the shrinking of the self-interested ego. And in "The Erectus Alternative," the fourth and final chapter in Kirkpatrick Sale's *After Eden*, there are useful and stimulating probings into the nature of human consciousness—not merely what we have lost, but also what may be more fully recoverable than we realize.

VI. Nowhere have I found this balance between political socialism and decentralist economy is an economy within the regenerative capacities of nature. Such an economy would be hugely frugal compared to what we now have. Forget Wal-Mart. Think mass transit, smaller and far more compact towns and cities. Think a huge proliferation of small farms and (to use a pleasant buzzword) eco-villages. Think the ecological decentralization of schools and a very welcome relaxation of compulsion—and an entirely new ecological orientation toward what gets taught in schools, sciences especially. Lots and lots of time outside, learning to recognize and identify the actual world we live in—crafts and languages, theater and art. Think lots of little sawmills, solar and wind gizmos, local cafes, coffee shops, and parks. Think a tremendous revitalization of local political engagement. In other words, the magnitude of decentralist folk initiative—educated, locally grounded, participatory, politically savvy—would serve as a political check on excessive centralist control.

Men, it seems, are in general more anxious than women in regard to the closer, more collective aspects of democracy. Men are full of posture about independence and individualistic strength, but they are, in the main, fearful of being considered unusual or different, disinclined toward intellectual eccentricity or spiritual iconoclasm, and therefore they are too often suckers for authoritative men who essentially tell them how to think and how to behave, all neatly fitted within the posture of "independence" and "strength." And this may well be one of the reasons why violence is so rife in the world. As the need for closer, more reflective and collective political consideration is demanded on Earth, men are reacting with hysterical, frightened rage. We are witnessing a global temper tantrum on the part of males. As this temper tantrum becomes bloodier and bloodier (and I mean to say here that a great deal of what I'm calling temper tantrum is shaped by both political ideology and religious mythology), the desperation and anger of the world's women will boil over. When this happens, when women have simply had enough and will tolerate no more mindless, bloody violence, is when the tipping point will be reached. We are not there yet. And it's anybody's guess how long it will take to get there—although we can see the rumbling dynamics of the "externalities"—climate change, systemic poverty, an obsession with

---

culture expressed with greater lucidity than in R. H. Tawney's *The Acquisitive Society*, pages 86 and 87. I quote from Tawney's book in "A Proper Balance," chapter 16 in *Nature's Unruly Mob: Farming and the Crisis in Rural Culture.*

"terrorism," and so on—and realize this clock is ticking louder and louder, faster and faster.

The great American historian Lewis Mumford said there were "traumatic institutions" embedded in civilization and that we are in the midst of global crises on their account.[2] The great British historian Arnold Toynbee said there are two "diseases" of civilization, Class and War, and our task is to rid civilization of them.[3] Whether we might call such a cleansed system "civilization" is actually rather unimportant. What *is* important is that a radically deepened consciousness of libertarian, ecological, democratic socialism cannot proceed without a corresponding spiritual commitment to radical servanthood and radical stewardship. With such a commitment, we may safely and freely explore a wholly new world. Therefore we may truly say that what we typically identify as elements of global crisis—climate change, excessive consumption, militarism, species extinction, etc., etc.—rest on a melded civilized/religious worldview that permits and even encourages such seemingly limitless abuse. We may also say that the resolution of these crises requires a new and different spiritual understanding, an understanding that breaks out of two boxes simultaneously: the box of explicit religious fundamentalism and the box of civilizational self-containment. In the first box, the Age of the Mother is simply denied and God is purely Male. In the second box, civilization's inner power structure is held and controlled by male warrior energy and this control is believed to be normative. And although women have been steadily flooding into many areas previously deemed exclusively male—law, religion, politics, medicine, etc.—they have largely done so in accord with pre-established rules of conduct and outlook, essentially taking on the garb (and the requisite male "toughness") of the institutions into which they've been flooding. What's needed now is for women—not only women, but especially women—to break out of those boxes, publicly identify the traumatic institutions, propose cures for civilization's diseases, and begin to thoroughly redirect public consciousness toward a deeper and gentler spirituality.

It is my hope that the world's women will prove more than equal to the challenge. If women aren't equal to the challenge, it'll be either aristocratic restoration or disaster beyond the scope of imagination. But thinking ourselves "civilized" has rendered us ethically sluggish if not altogether comatose. It's time to awaken not merely to our political responsibilities, but also to our *spiritual* outrage.

NOTES

1. Thoreau, *Walden*, 89.
2. Mumford, *Pentagon*, 199.
3. Toynbee, *Civilization*, 23.

3

A Little Early

I HAVE A FRIEND who used to work for the biggest public sector union in Wisconsin, although he now consults for a think tank that explores the deepening of democracy. Occasionally he sends me copies of papers he receives, and sometimes I even read them. Once in a while I send him a few pages of ill-tempered opinion in reply. I confess to a certain impatience with "workshops" and "focus groups." Perhaps my long retreat in the woods has made me into something of a snob or a cranky and cretinous sourpuss.

However, I really *want* to believe there's a deepening of democratic sensibility going forward in this country, even globally. But while I *want* to believe it, I keep having this troubled feeling that it's supremely easy to misidentify consumer trends as democratic consciousness. By "consumer trends" I mean not only a common standardization produced by corporate name brands, pop music, and the proliferation of all manner of hip gadgets and cool electronic gizmos, I also mean the massive consolidation of school systems with their seemingly endless extracurricular activities, by organized everything, and by a subtle, all-pervading compulsory coddling (surrounding by an amorphous anxiety or fear) by which a kind of mushy togetherness becomes psychologically normative, all of that togetherness thoroughly nestled in the comforts of Empire affluence.

We have become a nation of soft little puppies, in other words, whose physical symbol, we might even say, is rampant obesity. And, while there are no die-hard authoritarians in puppyland, except the AM radio talking-head types, its "democracy" has not met any real-life challenges, either. Or, insofar as there are real-life challenges to be met—global warming and climate change, AIDS, toxins, a widening chasm between rich and poor, rampant militarism in the service of "strategic interests," the maintenance of Empire corporations instead of local economies, etc., etc.—the latest

19

iPod might have a barely intelligible song that tells us all about it. We are afloat in comfort and affluence, in other words, in an economic system busily building and intensifying disasters, and so our Happy Talk about democracy is not exactly to be trusted. Democracy is not just comforting electoral procedure. Much less is it shopping-mall affluence. If the democratic impulse does not deepen into ethical understanding and spiritual conviction, it will become an increasingly empty formality, as destitute politically as it is likely to become economically.

In "Temper Tantrum," I said we needed libertarian, ecological, democratic socialism. In this essay I would like to explore (insofar as I am able) the "ecological" part of that package. My premise is that we are at a crisis, not simply in the history of civilization, but as regards the perpetuation of civilization itself; and to achieve a democratic resolution to this crisis, without reverting to explicit aristocratic governance or falling into the pit of global devastation, requires facing into and facing up to the inherently undemocratic and unecological characteristics within inherited civilization. Either we will have civilization or we will have democracy, but we probably cannot have both. Using ecology as a conceptual tool, I will try to explain what I mean.

Because ecology is the web of relationships in and between natural systems, what matters most, conceptually and practically, is the relationship between those natural systems and ourselves, especially between nature and the human economy—if, by "human economy," we mean to include weapons of mass destruction invented and deployed, as it were, to backstop rival political configurations of human economy. ICBMs are in North Dakota silos to protect Wal-Mart, General Motors, and IBM. And, because such institutions are part and parcel of that matrix we call civilization, we can confidently say that civilization has now developed to the point—with its "traumatic institutions" (Mumford) and "diseases" (Toynbee)—where ecology's most deadly enemy is civilization. Precisely as civilization has attained something akin to global supremacy, global ecology starts to systematically falter. Can there really be any doubt about the linkage?

Yet this linkage is more than most of us can accept or swallow. We have been raised in an atmosphere, both intellectually and spiritually, where "civilization" exceeds even religion as the means by which humanity has leveraged itself out of an undesirable primitivity and achieved a "civilized" ambience of culture. Civilization might even have made us "ready" for Christianity. (Why do we think "Christian pagan" an utter and ridiculous oxymoron, a contradiction in terms, while "civilized Christian" is a concept whose feet we kiss?) The Christian religion has largely asserted its priority of not being "of this world," and so its self-appointed task has been to prepare souls for a possible life on the far side of death. Shaping human conduct on this side of death has been largely the job of civilized institutions—government, the military, the economy, schooling. And, since civilized institutions have claimed to be utterly superior in relation to noncivilized cultural forms (the latter were invariably torpid, brutish, backward, and deficient in one way or another), the civilized duty was to overpower such forms, free their occupants from their intellectual limitations and spiritual captivity, and introduce them, forcibly if necessary, to a superior way of life. In America we have had such slogans as "Better dead than Red" (applied both to Indians and to any left-of-center political point of view) and "We had to destroy the village in order to save it" (the aphorism, epigraph, and epitaph of the American war on Vietnam). These slogans exactly and succinctly express the mission of civility, *civis* squeezing the vital juice out of *pagus*, of smashing the red village into smoldering smithereens.

So the ecological crisis is symptom and consequence of demented civilized hubris in its globalized mode. That is, to address the ecological crisis requires addressing its cause, and its cause is civilization. And, while various technofixes are no doubt necessary, technofix as an ideology represents a civilized ambulance crew, a vigorous adrenalin-driven gang of first responders. It is not to be taken seriously as structural corrective. There is no technical fix for this global crisis. The "fix" that's needed, the only "fix" possible, if we are to have a humane, ecological, and democratic future, is repentance of our impulse towards supremacy and a restoration of cultural earthiness.

Now I know that "repentance" drips with evangelistic moral muck. But it's not my fault that the concept we need has been so abused and corrupted. (Should we be surprised that it has been so misused?) Yet the civilized mentality is one of such unmitigated, convicted superiority that only its implosion, its conscious and deliberate withdrawal from that deadly posture of superiority, is an adequate precondition for reorienting the human project on Earth (whatever it may be) from universal disaster toward something resembling ecologically humble humanitarianism. Repentance requires such implosion: either psychospiritual implosion or military-industrial explosion.

The core energy within civilization is not and never has been democratic. Its core energy is and has been righteous superiority, an expansive, vigilant, conquering power consciously intending to dominate and exploit. Therefore we can say that the advance of democracy, its deepening both culturally and ecologically, depends unconditionally on the implosion of superiority as a repentant precondition. Now one may rightly apply these dynamics of domination and exploitation, as well, to the precivilized hunter and even, in a far more ambiguous and qualified way, to the gatherer. Self-interested aggression and domination didn't magically emerge with the first king or city. The core energy within civilization had to come from somewhere—it didn't simply invent itself out of thin air—and it is sentimental to assert that precivilized cultures were free of righteous superiority. Perhaps the core impulse comes simply from our biological nature. We all live by eating, and we eat from living things, both plant and animal. To eat we kill and take. We need clothing and shelter, and as our individual lives are in reciprocal complexity with whatever larger economy we were born into, we grow up with a sense of the normative, recognizing perhaps, but having a moral distance from, the ecological impact caused by the satisfaction of our hunger. As biological beings who live by eating, we have to acknowledge the willful aggression expressed in the taking of other life forms for our sustenance, as well as group protection of an area that "belongs" to us.[1]

The noncivilized person came home to a community, to a village, to a common life differentiated primarily by age and by gender. The civilized person comes home to a class identity, to a city, to an abstracted life sustained by an amazing, even impenetrable web of institutionalized dependencies and structural aggressions largely hidden from view and whose crisis points are blandly reported as "news," usually from an "objective" or nationalistic point of view. We often feel psychologically detached from these crises, only rarely cognizant of any direct responsibility. To radically "simplify" one's life or to dissociate from the Empire system to any significant extent would be seen by family and friends as going off the deep

---

I. Mumford, in *The Myth of the Machine*, page 169, says "it was hunting that cultivated the initiative, the self-confidence, the ruthlessness that kings must exercise to achieve and retain command; and it was the hunter's weapons that backed up his commands ... with the ultimate authority of armed force: above all, the readiness to kill." This "readiness to kill" is exactly why male hunting and not female gathering must be held to primary account for rampant human dominance on Earth.

end. But I am not arguing here for some dreamy concept like "leaving the Earth a better place than I found it." Whether any human being has ever left the Earth "a better place" is dubious, at best. I am speaking, or trying to speak, ecologically. Living "sustainably" doesn't necessarily mean anybody is leaving the Earth "better." It simply means our taking is not ecologically ruinous. It is therefore self-evident that noncivilized peoples have had a far more benign impact on nature's ecology than civilized peoples—and by "noncivilized" I mean to include the traditional peasantry, even under the exacting expropriation of the aristocracy, for the peasantry largely shared with noncivilized peoples an economy of sufficiency and subsistence. Peasants remained within folk evolution, even if that evolutionary process was boxed in. But civilization breaks out of folk evolution, at first oppresses the folk community for reasons of resource expropriation, and then surpasses it entirely by means of utopian technologies that no longer need a folk-based producer class or community.

I am not, however, arguing for a cartoonish Yogi Bear subsistence or a diet of nuts and berries. But when the food on our plates has traveled anywhere from two to five thousand miles before being impaled by our dinner forks, we are eating a very civilized meal, a meal absolutely absurd in terms of ecology, energy efficiency, sustainability, nutrition, or the vitality of local agrarian culture. A glacier in Greenland melts so we can eat our California iceberg lettuce. The Seventh Fleet prowls the Persian Gulf so trucks, with refrigeration units, can haul that lettuce to our neighborhood Sam's Club, where, while we're at it, we can stock up on a variety of cheap consumer goods made in China, shipped on sea lanes guarded by our Navy.

I am not saying that noncivilized cultures were democratic, libertarian, ecological, or socialist. They may have had some "primitive" mixture of these elements, at some level; but I tend to accept that they were governed—culturally governed—primarily by tradition, some large proportion of which was determined by gender distinctions and a not-always-friendly psychology that goes with sharp distinctions in gender identity and turf control.

I suppose the question then is: if traditional peoples shared on the basis of village, ethnic, or tribal identity, doesn't it follow that universalist democratic aspiration is a product of civilization? A result precisely of a force that broke the self-imposed encapsulation of village life? The answer appears to be yes, although it is a yes surrounded by serious qualifications.

Insofar as civilization meant or produced Empire—and what else do names like Babylonia, Egypt, China, Greece, Rome, Spain, Britain, Turkey, Russia, Japan, or the United States imply?—human identity, human consciousness, was correspondingly expanded, or inflated, from village to empire dimensions. All these empires had their elites, their aristocracies. But only with rare exception did a democratic impulse come from the elites. Insofar as it did come from the elite class, its brand of democracy was largely restricted to its class. The Magna Carta.

So where did the deeper democratic impulse originate? It had to have come from the dispossessed, from the exploited and the abused. It contained revulsion toward the oblivious pride, cruelty, stolen wealth, and cultural arrogance of the elite. It yearned for freedom, for equality, for sharing, and for a commonwealth organized for the common good, and this common good in cultural terms is a harkening back to the egalitarianism of precivilized life. Insofar as any of these concepts became nominally integrated into a political system—and our American system is such a one—the trick for the elite was to legislate and govern in the direction of elite domination while simultaneously satisfying the electorate with the rhetoric and symbolic gestures of "democracy." To cite a single illustration, consider the passage of various Free Trade bills, that have helped to undermine domestic industries, undercut industrial unions, and plunge the nation into deeper and deeper debt, even as the rationale for passage was "freedom" and "prosperity."

With industrialization, a peculiar set of conditions was created for ordinary people. That is, the lower orders of society, peasants in particular, were previously not included in governance. The aristocracy represented both practical governance and metaphysical civilization. But with industrialization, the folk base of society, heavily engaged in subsistence production and modest self-provisioning, was compelled, coerced, and finally lured into an increasingly abstract consumerist mode of life. Peasants were forced off the land. Despite bloody battles over unionization, the overall economy was becoming increasingly imperial, and the domestic affluence so generated, in concert with the stunning religious sense of superiority historically embedded in Euro-American Christianity—a sense of superiority fully infiltrated into and integrated with political consciousness— created an American working-class personality powerfully aligned with civilized values through the medium of righteous nationalism heavily tainted by racism and religious superiority.

"Democracy" became power politics on a mass scale, with "interest groups" grasping for the goodies political control provided. For the Democratic Party, we might say this sort of "democracy" reached its zenith at the Chicago convention in 1968, a "zenith" from which the party has never recovered. The fat unions of the white working class crashed and burned when Mayor Daley and the counterculture collided in Grant Park. The winner of '68 was the Republican Party of Nixon, Reagan, and the Bushes. When white working-class unions, racist and reactionary, hating civil rights and supporting the assault on Vietnam, exalted as angry cops beat antiwar hippies, their struggle for democracy was over. They had already integrated their identity with imperialism and, correspondingly, with the project of civilization.[II] By the early 1980s it was explicit—Democrats for Reagan—as the Great Communicator launched covert wars on the dispossessed of Central America, cut taxes on the rich, initiated "three strikes and you're out," began a process of deregulation, and hugely magnified the national debt—all the while pretending the Republican Party was the party of "family values" and "fiscal responsibility."

Amaury de Riencourt, in a 1957 book entitled *The Coming Caesars*, said it's excess of democracy that produces Caesars. Amaury de Riencourt (and Oswald Spengler before him) was wrong. It's a *shrinking back from democracy*, a withdrawal from servanthood and stewardship, that produces an imaginary, fake "democracy" ruled by con men, spin doctors, and advertisers. It's not that democracy has failed. The question is: what kind of spiritual, cultural, and economic base is needed for the flowering of real democracy? Democracy can only be as healthy as the spiritual economy out of which it arises.

The patient may be unwell, but it's still a little early for a funeral.

II. See Mark Kurlansky's *1968: The Year that Rocked the World.*

4

Absolutely Scandalized

IN MY *GREEN POLITICS Is Eutopian*, especially in the single longest essay ("Their Fearful Energies"), the subject pondered is centralization
versus decentralization. Or, to put it differently, civilization versus folk
culture. The stance in that essay—that a vital balance is needed—is one I
still adhere to, although not without a deep sense of ambiguity. The question is whether civilization has a hidden, deeper, historic purpose than
merely the forced expansion to global scale of its "traumatic institutions."
If civilization *does not* have such a hidden, deeper purpose, then its "traumatic institutions" will eventually reach their fullest expression, and it'll
either be catastrophe or aristocratic restoration. Democracy, as a political
aspiration potentially capable of incorporating the large-scale in a way
that also protects and nourishes the small-scale, will die or, at the very
least, atrophy in the compulsory direction of folk-culture retrogression
and peasant powerlessness.

So, if civilization has an overarching positive purpose, what is it?
Well, we could say it is a sense of the whole, global awareness in various
manifestations, epitomized, perhaps, by the famous photograph of Earth
from a space craft. But it is also possible that these manifestations of
global awareness are unintended by-products of a core drive representing
aggressive expansion and predatory discipline—a drive to "conquer" both
nature and all noncivilized peoples, and to impose a certain amorphous,
incoherent utopian ideal on all subjugated people and places. But if one
successfully conquers the whole by means of aggression and predation, is
this any different than the biblical warning against gaining the world at
the expense of one's soul?

Another way to approach this question (though one can only go so
far with it) is to ask whether there is some inherent flaw or limitation
within folk culture that civilization holds the promise of correcting. This

approach contains, obviously, two separate hypotheses—the possible "inherent flaw" within folk culture, and the potential "correcting promise" held by civilization. It needs to be said, however, that even if folk culture has an inherent flaw, it does not necessarily follow that civilization contains the necessary corrective.

The tack I took in "Their Fearful Energies"—as, indeed, in much of my writing over the past thirty years—is that folk culture's flaw, its limitation, lies in its gender rigidity and tribal exclusion, two traits that seem to ensure suppression of women and conflict between groups. By breaking into and breaking up the deeply embedded patterns of folk culture (perhaps by "smashing up . . . social structures in order to extract the element of labor from them," as Karl Polanyi famously put it in *The Great Transformation*[1]), civilization forcibly replaces folk structures, folk behaviors, with civilized constructs. For children, organized schooling replaces integration into the traditional informality of village life. The factory replaces craft. Consumerism replaces subsistence. Identification with the formally organized, including the exactingly organized State, replaces extended family and village loyalty. (Even with all its ambiguities, how else are we to understand the difference between the Farmers Alliance of the late nineteenth century, defeated electorally as the People's Party in 1896, and the industrial unions from, say, 1930 until 1970, defeated by their very success: defeated in their *democratic* purpose by having "outgrown" their folk psychology, their folk identity, and by having aligned themselves with civilized power and empire presumption? In 1896, folk culture was defeated at the civilized polls. In 1968, white industrial unions were defeated by their systemic atrophy of folk culture consciousness and their self-inflicted embrace of predatory nationalism with its racist undercurrents.)

Civilization globally supreme is only another way of stating the corresponding universal degradation of folk culture. This is our historic situation. We see that as folk culture everywhere undergoes cultural corruption, with the breaking down of traditional folkways, we are also compelled to recognize that the technological substitutes forcibly constructed and imposed by civilization are woefully lacking in ecological, cultural, or spiritual coherence. Thus we have a many-headed Global Crisis. Civilization in the past could be oblivious of the debt owed to folk culture stability and strength; but folk strength was sapped by armed conquest, the overthrow of subsistence, and the imposition of technological industrialization. And so civilization, as folk culture atrophies, is more and more devoid of its previous ecological buffer and cultural supports, even as we can see through its remaining high-culture disguises, embellishments, and justifications (that grow thinner and thinner) to its underlying predatory skeleton.

What do we see? We see a raw, bleak, will-to-power energy with incredibly deadly technologies grasping for cultural or religious justifications. With Korea, Vietnam, Iraq, and Afghanistan, we see "democracy," the "free world," and "Christian" triumphalism as the American rationale grasped or proffered. The movies that depict a killer robot hidden in human form represent a mass media metaphor for this very process. Civilization is programmed for violent predation. It has a fanatic automaton living in its soul, camouflaged by every possible humane rationalization.[1]

So if civilization contains a corrective for the flaw or limitation within folk culture, what *is* that civilized corrective? It surely is not a set of "traumatic institutions" radically compacted in the image of a killer robot, even if that killer robot likes to think of itself as the bearer of enlightenment. If the classical "ambience of civility"—high art, lofty philosophical principals, and all the rest—is only the stage scenery hiding backstage brutal aggression, why do we persist in insisting that the scenery *is* civilization? Are we slyly implying that the "ambience of civility" *justifies* the steady destruction of folk culture? That folk culture is so deeply flawed that only its extermination, its utter crushing, is capable of freeing humanity from the gnarly unseemliness of repugnant backwardness? This is completely untenable. It always was untenable. It's also very late to come to this awareness.

Global warming, climate change, rampant overpopulation, reckless consumption of Earth's resources, deadly militarism, apocalyptic weaponry, deadly toxins—all this and more are the consequences of globalized civilization. Unless we *look* unflinchingly at the "traumatic institutions" and "diseases" of civilization, and *repent* of their perpetuation, we are only dabbling. And dabbling means perpetuation. In the past, it was possible

---

1. See Noam Chomsky's *The New Military Humanism*. On pages 11 and 12, Chomsky says, in his usual ironic style, "The self-described bearers of enlightenment happen to be the rich and powerful, the inheritors of the colonial and neocolonial systems of global dominion: they are the North, the First World." If Wendell Berry is America's leading moralist arguing in behalf of rural culture and small-scale farming, Noam Chomsky holds a similar status in the realm of foreign policy.

to get away with such dabbling. But a very grim reality is closing in on us, and playing a conceptual shell game with "civilization" (like George W. Bush's "civilization versus terrorism") is intellectually corrupting and spiritually criminal.

But we're still not answering the basic question: is there a deeper purpose in civilization? Well, insofar as civilization asserts an *intentional* deeper purpose, I say it does not have one. Its conscious (though seldom honest or freely admitted) purpose is control, expansion, consolidation, power, and exploitation—what the dictionary calls *Realpolitik* or what Mumford calls "traumatic institutions"—even as the civilized elite have always felt a need to justify their predatory actions with moral, philosophical, or religious assertions.

But we are not fully governed by intentionality. There are unintended consequences and subtle, hidden motives. There are contrary, subversive drives. I would say that democracy, as a doctrine of human equality, is in part an unintended consequence of civilized expansionism. That is, as more and more people were squeezed out of subsistence livelihoods and compelled to enroll in civilized institutions, especially as these institutions operate under a theoretical ethic of equality, "democracy" becomes a byword of contemporary consciousness. And insofar as the women's movement is an extension of democracy—political suffrage, feminism—it, too, is an unintended consequence. These are unintended consequences antithetical to the premise, what the CIA calls "blowback." That is, democracy so far has not recognized that it is less a popular extension of civilization's elite trajectory than it is civilization's antithesis. When you really think about it, "democratic civilization" is a monstrous term, a deadly oxymoron of historic proportions, for it "democratizes" diseases and traumatic institutions while wearing a cloak of cultural and religious superiority in order to justify its economic imperialism. Concepts like "Manifest Destiny" and "American Exceptionalism" convey quite well the essence of that monstrous fusion—"democracy" merged with civilization. "The coming Caesars."

But it has been the consistent predatory designs of civilization, its relentless expansionism, its intensified lethality, and its mounting global "externalities" that have necessitated the formulation of a humane and ecological alternative, for once having glimpsed the global, having tasted it, we don't wish to shrink back to precivilized folk dimensions. But this is also a conundrum. The global has been achieved by brutal, predatory aggression; how do we sustain a sense of the global (both humane and ecological) without the predation? This is especially difficult when the conventional standard of living absolutely depends on an economy of predation packed in an accrued mentality of privilege and entitlement. This is the historical point, the spiritual hinge, humanity has reached. This is our present dilemma, or at least it is one way to formulate it.

Class and war must go, says Toynbee. Civilization's traumatic institutions must be clearly identified and dissolved, says Mumford. That means we need a politics with an absolutely new kind of ethical clarity and spiritual courage—the courage to be nonviolent, the courage to equalize wealth, the courage to share, the courage to embrace nature rather than to fight or "conquer" it, the courage to recognize and affirm the essential humanity of every human person irrespective of sex or race. If civilization achieved global dimensions by means of righteous violence, utilizing war to create economic inequality and divisions of class, how do we sustain global intimacy without the underlying or overarching structural violence? A new courageous politics must at all times shun and avoid false formulation. It must truly renounce pandering. It must be willing to face the false mystique of civilization and unflinchingly identify its historic predatoriness, while also being vulnerable to the vicissitudes of equality in a world of ecological limitation and resource finitude. This clearly means a spiritual distancing from the idolatries of technocracy, from the remorselessness of Progress, a reorientation toward a simpler, hardier, truer, more fulfilling spirituality, a turn from the tower of Babel to Arcadia, perhaps, at any rate a radical decentralization with a hugely modified industrial infrastructure carefully calibrated to ecological tolerances and cultural stability.

Folk culture will reconstitute itself through this spiritual funnel. It will resurrect itself. But it will be a new sort of folk culture, consisting of the very best of civilization with the deeper groundedness of precivilized cultures. I am speaking here *as if* this will happen. At the deepest levels of hope, I will it to happen. I wish to live the rest of my life in the manner and spirit of it happening. As I have said elsewhere, the kingdom of God, as propounded by Jesus, contains an ethic of radical stewardship and radical servanthood, and it provides an alternative organizing principle to the predatory selfishness of civilization. But this alternative organizing principle requires a spiritual, cultural, and political conversion. And part of our heritage of religious perversity is that "conversion" has been defined by such exceeding narrowness, so rigorously confined to a rigidly drawn, otherworldly, "spiritual" parameter, that conversion in the manner I am here advocating provokes paroxysms of religious apoplexy. Jesus, with much alarm, is piously snatched back from any such worldly contamination. That is to say, much of what we call "religious" claims for itself a status as semidivine gatekeeper to the holy. Defining Jesus is the job of the church, as is explaining the real ("not of this world") meaning of the kingdom of God. Consistent otherworldliness guarantees that the churches, almost without exception, drift along with the political status quo, and few challenges or rebukes will be forthcoming from the pulpits. (Or, if there are rebukes, they are couched in long-suffering, not-of-this-world moral superiority larded with spiritual hopelessness.)

Religion, largely, *is* an opiate, a spiritual narcotic, and, as such, it resists and objects to the "kingdom" servanthood and stewardship of libertarian, democratic, ecological socialism. *This* world is fallen and doomed; religion must do its scripted part—literally—to prepare its followers for the catastrophic inevitable, even as it may carp and complain. Christianity in particular is drugged with paradoxical doctrines of spiritual passivity and of forcibly supporting the use of the state as an aggressive agent for Christian triumphalism. The soldier clears the ground for the missionary. The sword hacks open a path for the cross. Christianity, in this sense, has been the Great Enabler, the codependent of predation. Such deepening of democracy as we do have comes largely from those who have slipped out of the coils of the religious drug while recognizing (at some level) the ethical liberation threaded through its basic scriptures—slipping out of Augustine's stern and pious rationalizations in favor of the revolutionary openness of Jesus.

The transformation we are entering touches every aspect of human life. Either unimaginable disaster, aristocratic restoration, or the eutopian transformation of human culture in every conceivable dimension.[II] If some Intelligence is shepherding these eutopian sheep, it is a shepherding of awesome risk, courage, confidence, and audacity. To fail to participate in this effort would be, on our part, a cosmic crime. We might even call it the Second Fall. Or, alternatively, if it should prove to be successful,

---

II. For a systematic treatment of these themes, see *Living Beyond the "End of the World"* by Margaret Swedish. Her writing is fresh and conversational, and it conveys an oddly invigorating sense of urgency.

it might be called the Second Coming of Christ—though lots of church leaders will be absolutely scandalized by a female savior.

NOTES

1. Polanyi, *Great*, 164.

5

Except for You

THE CONSCIOUSNESS THAT SATURATES our daily lives is largely devoid of what it would mean or what it would take to live "ecologically." For all our talk of ecology and ecological living, we are overwhelmingly a bunch of abstracted airheads and ungrounded gasbags. We have surpassed "sustainability" to such a degree that our naive talk about achieving "simplicity" is actually embarrassing. We jabber about "Creation," but we expend almost no mental energy exploring what that truly means—except, perhaps, for swatting a politically correct "Green" shuttlecock back and forth in a vigorous game of technofix badminton. "Cap and trade."

I am not here so much criticizing the supercivilized corporate Right, those who believe gated communities are proof of God's predestined Calvinist tendencies, but, rather, the liberal Left that seems to believe a Prius is a divine ecochariot or a basket full of recyclable bottles proof of Green salvation. It is the latter folks who have largely cornered the prevailing understanding of "ecological," and the poor "ecological" inmate is getting terribly anorexic.

"Right" and "Left" in this country are for the most part the respective camps of Empire and Empire Lite, of unhesitant greedy righteousness versus a mildly guilty, self-satisfied affluence. It's possible the latter would move beyond compact fluorescent bulbs if the political space opened sufficiently, but it is not opening sufficiently because (at least in part) we all have a tight grip on what the Standard of Living means to each of us, and we are in no mood to let go of that grip or promote policies that endanger that grip—and that includes voting (or, rather, not voting) for serious Green candidates like, for instance, Ralph Nader. (Which corporations are your retirement funds caught up in? Or did they evaporate in the financial meltdown of 2008?) We are all like the wit who, when confronted by the question "When is a house too big?" answered unhesitatingly, "When it's bigger than mine."

The stock market went up and up and up since 1980—at one point over 1,200 percent beyond that 1980 benchmark—and its ascension was universally celebrated, even worshipped, in the newscasts. (The National Public Radio program "Marketplace" plays lively, happy music when the stock market goes up, doleful tunes when it goes down.) For the stock market to plunge (as it did in October 2008) was absolutely dreadful, something indicative of cosmic failure, even of evil. We therefore recognize only the most tenuous connections between a "healthy" stock market—that is, a steadily ascending one, indicative of a constantly growing economy, at least for a class of wealthy investors and aggressive speculators—and brutal ecological consequences. Al Gore, at the conclusion of his movie *An Inconvenient Truth*, after the slick PowerPoint presentation of Global Warming and Climate Change facts, remains firmly committed to a vision of a "booming" economy.

It's not that an ecological economy would be devoid of vitality. Not at all. But it would not, could not, and will not be "booming" in any way comparable to the industrial/electronic/financialized economy we have known. To say or imply that it would be is to pander to blindness, to our selfishness and fear. To engage in such pandering is to prolong and compound the crisis; for, at some level, while every thinking person knows such an assertion (of affluent continuation) is hollow and false, it provides a synthetic fig leaf by which to keep shame hidden and repentance at bay. A growing economy is supposedly a good and necessary thing; we only need it tweaked by Green technofix. Therefore I need not change my way of life. What's needed is a retooling of technology precisely so no real lifestyle change or spiritual transformation is necessary. This is the role that "Green" is now assigned: find us ways to continue to be alpha utopian in a world sickening unto death due to the accrued externalities of alpha utopianism.

I am far more inclined to accept the view of James Howard Kunstler, who says when oil goes, when we're seriously into the downslope of Peak Oil, the magician who jerks the tablecloth from under our affluence will spread dirty silverware and broken china all over the floor. Thanks to cheap oil, we've had a very opulent free lunch and subsistence skills have largely died. Empire hubris meshed with willful incompetence is about to come face to face with Hunger. "Culture," says Helena Norberg-Hodge in her wonderful book *Ancient Futures*, "plays a far more fundamental role in shaping the individual than I had previously thought."[1] She says this in regard to her deep and sustained exposure to the Ladakhi culture of Kashmir. But here I mean to use that assertion to say that we, as a society, are living in a state of ecological avoidance and spiritual denial shaped by the ecological obliviousness of a civilized and industrialized mental hegemony. Our brains have been blowdried by otherworldly salvation, by the ideology of Progress, by "cheap" energy. Our connections with all prior forms of ecological economy have been brutally severed by the unhesitating superiority of civilized hubris in an industrial, electronic mode. This blind, oblivious superiority has become our "culture," our way of being in the world. And when this blithe arrogance crumbles around us, what will we do?

It is hardly possible to overstate the extent to which the civilized bulldozer has scraped the cultural landscape free of subsistence aptitudes and self-provisioning orientations. What once were self-sustaining native cultures on this continent—some fully intact only one hundred fifty years ago—are now demoralized, drunken enclaves boxed in on reservations, hoping that a new casino will lift them out of poverty and squalor. What were once self-sufficient African cultures, brutally uprooted into American plantation slavery, then (for a few generations) permitted to eke out a bare agrarian subsistence under a predatory sharecropper system, are now stuck in inner-city crime-and-drug ghettoes, shunned, feared, and hated by much of white society. And European peasants, having passed through the small-farm phase of the Jeffersonian vision, squeezed or lured off farms in favor of industrial jobs and suburban living, now work at Wal-Mart for minimum wage and no health benefits. Our prisons and jails are packed, as it were, to the supermax, largely with people who've found some solace in drugs.

"Democracy" in a mass society, in huge political entities like our contemporary nation-states, is largely a slick, clever, highly postured game of electoral salesmanship. Without a deep and dedicated commitment to libertarian ecological socialism, such democracy as there is will steadily shrivel and wilt as the material conditions for wide-spread affluence disappear, as violent conflict ("civilization versus terrorism") accelerates the political infiltration of explicit authoritarian tendencies. Empire hubris will become more frantic and fanatic as the internal techno-"culture" steadily breaks down.

The primary imagery provided by slick magazines, television ads, and political rhetoric—and these images simply dominate our consciousness, except for the few people who deliberately shut them out—keeps us corralled in expectations of restored affluence and ongoing abundance. Despite some scary books (like Kunstler's *The Long Emergency*) and an occasional somewhat scary movie (like Gore's *An Inconvenient Truth)*, there are virtually no public venues for engaging the radical changes coming at us. Taxes dare not be raised, especially on the rich ("class warfare"), and gas-tax monies will only grudgingly be used for mass transit, and then in as constricted a way as possible ("socialism"). We will bust the illegal immigrants working in meat-packing plants, and spend billions on cops and walls to prevent Mexicans from crossing the border illegally, but there is no real debate, no substantial discussion, on how NAFTA impoverishes small Mexican farmers and forces them into economic desperation. Insofar as the Right is even willing to discuss Global Warming—to them it apparently remains merely an academic theory, at which they scoff and sneer, often calling it a hoax—it is only as an economic trigger by which to insist on the commissioning of new nuclear power plants. Nothing is to impede Growth. Nothing is to impugn our God-given Standard of Living. Only naive, romantic fools would call for a scaling back in energy usage, plead for an increase in localized food production, dream of a tight network of trains and busses publicly owned and operated, or dare to call for a decentralized educational system that would create schools with more freedom, less compulsion, and a keen orientation toward local ecology.[1]

We are all so caught up in and entangled with this bright, manic drive toward Progress, toward Civilized Living, that we are literally incapable of adequately recognizing its disastrous, destructive trajectory. Civilized Progress is supposedly a foolproof vehicle taking us to—if not exactly utopian perfection—then something as close to perfection as is humanly possible. It is God's car we're riding in, and we are God's chosen passengers. Those who dispute this are the spawn of the Evil One, spiritual degenerates whose subterranean linkage to primitivity, paganism, and all forms of uncivilized heathenism makes them ("We had to destroy the village in order to save it") dispensable and disposable. Better dead than Red.

I. See my "Preliminary Thoughts on Green Education," chapter 5 in *Green Politics Is Eutopian.*

It is this mentality of intellectual denial and spiritual indifference that is so utterly stunning. And the extent to which it has penetrated and saturated common consciousness is nothing short of awesome. (I know of no one who has traced its historical etiology more thoroughly and scrupulously than Lewis Mumford.) And this mentality's unwillingness to bend or change, even in the face of consequences of possible catastrophic magnitude, is truly amazing. How does one who grew up in it, and who is far from having shed its influence, penetrate the pathological dementia of its self-insistence? And how does one account for this bizarre convergence of developments that includes Peak Oil right along with Global Warming and Climate Change, rampant and even wild overpopulation along with the breakdown of subsistence cultures and the atrophy of subsistence skills, a worldwide peace movement simultaneous with surging militarism and terrorist violence, a rumbling women's movement as male retaliation is increasingly flagrant, a growing Green awareness even as Green politics seems to be losing what little traction it once had. Is some oblivious Fate playing games with us? Or is there (not so much above consciousness as deeply buried within it) a Spirit whose tender but relentless insouciance simply pushes through all our stubborn resistances, much as grass or flowers will pop right through the cracks in asphalt, precisely as the global situation becomes increasingly deadly and dire?

The most ecological human employment I can think of is household gardening. Since eating is our most fundamental need, getting food is our most fundamental task. An argument could be made, I suppose, for gathering and hunting as even more basically ecological. And, while I don't in principle dispute that, it is now, I think, simply impossible for human beings to reclaim such a form of culture. And although there may well be way too many of us humans presently alive on Earth—maybe upwards of four or five billion too many—nobody I know, including myself, is intending to voluntarily lighten the load. Gardening should be our model, our mantra, the place we go to pray and meditate. I am not, strictly speaking, a vegetarian. I believe in the efficacy of small-scale agriculture, of animals side-by-side with gardening, orchards, vineyards, and small fields—including subsistence hunting and fishing, where appropriate. I would like to be a member of a cooperative farm. But as my friend Dennis Boyer recently put it in a letter—well, first he said what's been "lost culturally" probably "can't be replaced as the entire context is gone." And then he said this: "I've learned that it is difficult to get people to yearn for things they have no concept of." I think this means, for the most part, that the script has pretty well been written. We have either absorbed adequate democratic impulses or we haven't. It's not possible to say, Hey! Remember small farms? Remember gardening? Most people haven't a clue what's meant, implied, or demanded by the loss of subsistence skills.

The pace is accelerating in a monumental, life-changing ride toward historic phase change. We have already entered the chamber of transformation. The kinds of spiritual practice that, in my estimation, provide the greatest discernment and lucidity are sustained meditation, gardening, sewing and knitting, caring for the aged, the ill or the handicapped, building a simple, sturdy house, splitting firewood. Chop wood and carry water, just as ancient Buddhist texts encourage. Love Spirit with all your heart, soul, strength, and mind, and love your neighbor (including the "neighbor" who is your officially designated enemy) as you love yourself. Put down the sword and take up the hoe. Abandon private property and live cooperatively. Turn spiritual principle into political conviction.

How hard it is to stop our sleepwalking! How drugged we are with civilized mythology and religious salvationism! But Spirit pushing up through the cracks in our mental asphalt is deaf to our insincere whining. It's time for the Daughter. She will not be stopped, even by those who toy with the evil power of thermonuclear weapons—in underground silos, in bombers, in submarines, and perhaps in satellites. She is coming to sweep up those deadly toys and to disarm the boys who play with them. She is coming to offer every soldier a hoe in exchange for his rifle, every general a servant's job instead of troop command, every politician a composting toilet to maintain, and every Wall Street executive a nurse's aide apprenticeship.

Do you want to get with the program? If you have two coats, give one away. Unimaginable blessings lie in wait. This is a resurrection almost no one is anticipating. Except for you, dear reader. Except, perhaps, for you.

NOTES

1. Norberg-Hodge, *Ancient*, 5.

6

An Epilogue to Hissy Fits

M<small>Y WIFE</small> S<small>USANNA</small> <small>FOUND</small> Helena Norberg-Hodge's *Ancient Futures* in a thrift store, bought it, read it, loved it, and passed it on to me. I was in the midst of writing these little essays and into the fourth or fifth before I picked up Helena's book. The story line of *Ancient Futures* is simple. The author, a Swedish linguist, went to Ladakh, in Kashmir, in 1975, began to learn the language, returning for extended periods.[1] She arrived in time to see Ladakhi culture function in its traditional way (heavily influenced by Tibetan Buddhism), and then see it begin to break down under the impact of "development" introduced from, through, and by India.

It would be easy to pick an entire basket of fruit from this wonderful book; but, for now, I'll confine myself to the opening paragraph of chapter 12, "Learning the Western Way":

> No one could deny the value of real education, that is, the widening and enrichment of knowledge. But today education has become something quite different. It isolates children from their culture and from nature, training them instead to become narrow specialists in a Westernized urban environment. This process is particularly striking in Ladakh, where modern schooling acts almost as a blindfold, preventing children from seeing the context in which they live. They leave school unable to use their own resources, unable to function in their own world.[1]

This strikes me exactly where I live. It describes precisely ("School is a place to forget traditional skills and, worse, to look down on them"[2]) my educational experience at two one-room elementary schools in my rural

---

1. For a compacted summation of Helena's Ladakhi experience, see her Foreword to my *Nature's Unruly Mob*.

township, high school in a town twelve miles away, and not quite two full years at a state university in Wisconsin.

Ladakhi culture, however, goes back time out of mind. It had a richness and complexity far, far greater than the nearly brand-new rural culture I grew up in. My father, at age nineteen, bought a "brush forty" in 1931 and began to make a small dairy farm with grubhoe, dynamite, horses, stoneboat, and his own muscles until, almost exactly fifty years later, the farm was sold out of the family. (The people who bought it failed and also sold. Crops are still taken off the fields, but it no longer is a functional farm.) As different in historical depth as these two cultures were (though my parents were, to some degree, in an ancient stream of European peasant self-provisioning), it is astonishing, sobering, and frightening to see how vulnerable each culture was to the enchantments and encroachments of "development." The transformation for both came fast and hard and mercilessly.

With the Amish in mind, I want to make what may seem like a digression. Chapter 6 of *Ancient Futures* is entitled "Buddhism: A Way of Life" and, besides explaining the Ladakhi saturation with Buddhist principles, Helena Norberg-Hodge also relates a time (she was present) when the Dalai Lama came to visit—a prolonged festive preparation, people streaming in by the thousands from the countryside for the week-long teaching, the air "charged with intense devotion, and yet amazingly at the same time there was almost a carnival atmosphere."[3] Joking, picnics, children playing everywhere. A young French Buddhist in attendance was "shocked," according to the author. "'These people are not serious. I thought they were supposed to be Buddhists,' he said scornfully."[4] Helena Norberg-Hodge then goes on to explain how deeply the habits and practices of Buddhist teaching saturated the culture—so saturated, in fact, that the people were largely unfamiliar with a special time specifically set aside for concentrated, intense devotion. The pattern of their lives was already gentle, calm, attentive, and warm.

I, as a distant and removed outsider, wish to embrace both the French Buddhist's scorn and the Swedish linguist's defense. That is, if the Ladakhis' spiritual practice had had that element the young Frenchman found so lacking—greater critical mindfulness, perhaps—Ladakhi culture might have been capable of resisting the allurements of "development." I realize the allusion to the Amish is ambiguous, for the resistance the Amish continue to put up against "development," while based on a very strong sense of community, cannot exactly be said to originate from "mindfulness" in the Buddhist sense—though neither would I say there are no resemblances or overlays. (It would be an intriguing study for a person with appropriate skills and adequate sensitivity.)

Allow me one more tenuous digression. Only yesterday I had the unexpected opportunity to page through a coffee table book on Tibetan Buddhism, reading almost none of the text. Instead, I gazed intently at the photographs. Most of the pictures were of formal festivities, of artifacts, and of ranking personages in the religious hierarchy. After a while, I found it a relief to see photos of ordinary people practicing their devotions. I was then struck by my own sense of relief—somewhat puzzled by it—so I paid closer attention to the contrast between the photos of the ordinary people and those of the colorfully robed religious authorities. Very soon I realized I didn't like many of the faces of those authorities. They struck me as spiritual gangsters or religious politicians. There was something self-satisfied, smug, and sly about them, and it occurred to me that that ambience may also help explain why Ladakhi culture was so apparently defenseless in the face of "development"—its leadership was, perhaps, spiritually corrupt and psychologically arrogant. Capable of helping to sustain a *cultural* Buddhism, in the face of a real threat it was, however, clueless and lacking in true *spiritual* grit and competence. I say that tentatively. But I think it worth pondering. (Religious authorities invariably project a commanding presence from within an unthreatened ecclesiastical context; but rattle their cages and there'll be an abundance of acrid smoke and sizzled lightning provoked primarily by sudden fear and defensive posture.)

It occurs to me, too, that traditional Ladakhi Buddhism might qualify as a "civil religion." However, there's an ambiguity here. "Civil" is from the same Latin root as "civilization," a root meaning "city," and so the more accurate term for Ladakhi Buddhism might be "cultural religion." American Christian nationalism is, by comparison, properly designated a "civil religion" precisely because its nation-state patriotism has taken on attributes of religious devotion and spiritual fervor. On the other hand, a cultural religion would, in its fullest expression, be so deeply embedded in the everyday lives of the common people that no elite governing class would be necessary for its practice or perpetuation. (We can, perhaps, get a glimpse of this possibility in John 4:20–24.)

Anyway, all of this puts us back into the basic dilemma. What is it that's capable of enabling us, collectively, to resist the destructive blandishments of "development" in a civilizational mode? Tibetan Buddhism in Ladakh couldn't do it. The rural Wisconsin culture I grew up in couldn't do it. The Amish to a rather large extent *can* do it—their peculiar religious culture was forged in an atmosphere of persecution and resistance from the beginning—but their resistance seems largely predicated on a peculiar strand of biblical literalism combining male authority with fear of a dreadfully judgmental Father God, a stance we reject and refuse, a theology we find impossible to embrace. We may admire and even envy the Amish their capacity to resist, but they seem to have arrived at a niche resistance because of principles, values, or points of view the rest of us find intellectually impossible to embrace.

Perhaps the question might be asked differently. Is there any *ethical* progress in human history? If the answer is no, if we (collectively) are no more ethical than our ancient ancestors, and if we are (collectively) incapable of becoming more ethical, then (unless a "dark age" intervenes to provide a temporary reprieve) we are destined for cascading catastrophes, probably sooner rather than later. If the answer to the question of ethical progress is no, I see no evasion of the catastrophic conclusion, either in honest discussion or in the unfolding of events.

But if the answer to the question is yes, if there *is* ethical progress, we not only have to point it out and make it discernible to the intellect, we also have to account for its force, explain its etiology, get a grip on why it's so. My answer to this question (though I readily confess to many, many dark nights of the soul) is that Something bubbles in the hidden inner darkness of our being, individually and collectively. I do not, as a rule, call this Bubbling Something by the name "God" because "God" seems overwhelmingly a projected worship object, something that's relentlessly elsewhere and judgmentally transcendent even as lip service may be given to "God" as benevolently immanent. In fact, virtually our entire civilized psychology is not emotionally conversant with Spirit as sweetly indwelling. We may on occasion say it, but we rarely *feel* it, and we certainly don't live there. The word "God" is way too big, however, for me to say it is not recoverable as Spirit; but its present use is so overwhelmingly tinny and gilded, so falsely revered as semantic idolatry, that to utter the word is to set a room of tin mirrors vibrating and echoing with metallic clangor.

What Helena Norberg-Hodge says of Ladakhi children—"They leave school unable to use their own resources, unable to function in their own world"—could be said, as well, of most religious people who insist that their salvation, like their savior, is "not of this world." Their blindfold not only prevents them from seeing the *cultural* context in which they live, it also obliterates all earthly, earthy, and ecological aspects of their spirituality. Abstract schooling is a logical consequence of otherworldly religion or of otherworldly religion in league with civilizational impoundment. Whatever else "development" may be, it most certainly is also the secularized, utopian transmutation of otherworldly religious doctrine into an obsession with gizmos and gadgets, with a lustful craving for the cornucopia of a technological cargo cult. It is "preparing" us for an ideal and utopian future even as it coaxes us into betraying *this* ecological world and our eutopian life in it.

It seems that only a radically deepened spirituality can save us, a spirituality repeatedly touching into that Something bubbling in the hidden inner darkness of our being. If there is no such Something, where in the world do we imagine any "ethical progress" comes from? Or do we believe ethical progress is the cultural afterglow of electronic technology or civilized refinement?

NOTES

1. Norberg-Hodge, *Ancient*, 110.
2. Norberg-Hodge, *Ancient*, 111.
3. Norberg-Hodge, *Ancient*, 76.
4. Norberg-Hodge, *Ancient*, 76.

7

Rusty Ancient Hinges

I T OCCURS TO ME that something more could be said about the categories of "culture" and "civilization." Not that I can here add a lot to the
literature (like Brooks Adams' *The Law of Civilization and Decay*, Oswald
Spengler's *The Decline of the West*, or Amaury de Riencourt's *The Coming
Caesars*—all of which are based on a culture/civilization dynamic), but it's
my impression that this dynamic is fully operative in our lives, mostly below the level of consciousness.[1] Distinguishing culture from civilization is
not necessarily all that easy or simple. Partly it's not easy or simple because
of how we've been taught. That is, in school most of us were introduced
to "civilization" by studying art or "high culture." That is, we learned that
"culture" was the spiritual aura or ethereal emanation radiating out from
"civilization." And so, at one level, it may be more meaningful to talk about

I. An additional clarification of terms might be useful. Charles Beard, in his 1942
Introduction to *The Law of Civilization and Decay* (1896), says, on page xxxvii, that
Brooks Adams' "law" is a "formula which purports to describe the movement of human
society in history as from barbarism to civilization and back again." This is, Beard goes
on to say, an "adaptation" of a cyclical theory worked out by Giambattista Vico and later
elaborated by Oswald Spengler.

Spengler (see pages 24 and 28 of his *Decline*) says that, through a process of "organic
succession," Civilization (with a capital C) is the product, outcome, or "destiny" of Culture.
Or, as he also says, "The energy of culture-man is directed inwards, that of civilization-
man outwards."

De Riencourt seems quite close to Spengler. On page 10 of his Introduction, de
Riencourt also talks of "organic succession," and then he goes on to say Culture is "original creation" whereas Civilization is a "crystallization" based on "petrified stock forms,
but efficient in its mass organization."

While it is clarifying and useful to assimilate these vast categories, it is Mumford's
far more detailed history (especially in *The Myth of the Machine* and *The Pentagon of
Power*) that not only gives substance to these generalities, but also serves as a critical
corrective to the elements of ideological reaction that are there in Adams, Spengler, and
de Riencourt.

"high culture" and its affiliation with "civilization" versus "low culture" and its affiliation with—well, with what?

If low culture is the opposite of high culture, what's the opposite of civilization? Our modern political answer is "terrorism," but that seems totally useless for our primary discussion. (Although, as we shall see, it will have a way of revealing its significance.) The opposite of preindustrial civilization would be folk life. So, as opposed to opera, for instance, we would say folk music, opposite ballet, folk dance, and so forth. In addition—again, thinking preindustrially—these folk arts were overwhelmingly rural and agrarian. And, as everybody knows (or should know), the atrophy of folk art correlates to the atrophy of agrarian culture. (A lot of what's now called "folk music" consists of left-of-center political agitation in musical form, often quite skilled and media savvy. But it is not folk music in the "classical" sense.)

So we can say that the opposite of civilization is not "wilderness" (see Henry Nash Smith's *Virgin Land: The American West as Symbol and Myth* for an analysis of that issue) but, rather, agrarian culture or the peasantry. So if, in the ancient precivilized past, we were all earthy culture, we have now turned ourselves inside out and have become all city, all civilization. If we can, to some extent, align Spirit to culture, we can also correlate God with civilization. If Spirit moves freely and lissomely in the realm of culture, God stands rigid and glowering over civilization. And as people who have become so thoroughly and reflexively civilized, we find it extremely difficult to break out of transcendence and enter the realm of the immanent. We have an ancient and embedded fear of God; but we also intuit that affinity with Spirit is far more ethically demanding (though much less moralistic), and therefore our resistances to spiritual freedom are actually activated by our religious fear, as paradoxical as that may seem. Once we have accepted civilized identity, it becomes difficult to let go of that attachment in favor of evolutionary folk culture association.

Now (we are here bending towards George W. Bush's either/or of civilization versus terrorism), in the March 12, 2007, issue of *The Nation* there were two articles that help us with this civilization/culture dynamic. In one, Naomi Klein devotes a column to the accused terrorist Jose Padilla who, she says, has been so psychologically damaged by psychological torture, while held in U.S. custody, that he "sees his captors as protectors." He has become "furniture."[1] In the other article, Christian Parenti reviews a book on the Vietnam-era journalist Bernard Fall. This ends up being more an analysis of war correspondents—Parenti is one—and on why those "who go to war have more political capital than those who stay home." He goes on to talk about the "typical male lust to watch war," a "somewhat sadistic thrill" that generates an "ugly Stockholm syndrome logic" of identifying with one's protectors who are often the main "killers, rapists and arsonists." Conversely, says Parenti, if you "identify constantly with the victims, you could easily lose your nerve and grow totally sickened by the spectacle of fear and humiliation and waste." And then the clincher, your "safety and sanity" depend on empire, on continued and sustained identification with empire, even as one may be ethically revolted by empire's behavior—ethically revolted but politically incapacitated.[2] With the noncivilized so ferociously characterized as the repository of chaotic terror, we can easily see how the uncivilized can be linked to evil, to the demonic, or even to the Devil.

One of the things I am asserting in these polemics and provocations is that our ancient inheritance of noncivilized culture is in many ways exhausted. In 1790, for instance, the first American census showed that (of those counted) either ninety or ninety-five percent of citizens lived rurally and were engaged in some sort of agriculture. We are now down to one or two percent. So just as our American agricultural demographic has been turned upside down in the last 220 years, so the world as a whole has seen a similar change from rural subsistence and self-provisioning to urban commercial consumerism, from culture to civilization. We have abandoned our cultural birthrights for a stew of technological and bureaucratic pottage.

Now I know that India is not America and Bolivia is not Switzerland. So there are places where subsistence persists, where indigenous people have the cultural depth to resist "development," at least to some significant degree. The capacity of cultures to resist depends on lots of factors, including spiritual groundedness and religious unity. So it seems pretty obvious, for example, that some of the self-serving political hype about "Islamofascism" is either deliberate falsification or ideologically driven misidentification of unified cultural resistance to aspects of "development," a resistance articulated through the unifying medium of religious affiliation. By supporting dictators like the Shah of Iran or the Saudi royal family, the U.S. witlessly has reaped the reward of "blowback" created when dissent got channeled with increasing militancy into and through the mosque precisely because such dissent was denied expression in the civic arena. Since dissent couldn't be openly secular, it was forced into being secretly and militantly religious. Thus the Iranian revolution of 1979 identified the U.S. as the Great Satan, and the majority of the 9/11 hijackers were Saudi nationals. Many Islamists have been saying to rampant Western "development" what Nancy Reagan once told kids to say about drugs: Just Say No.

Western Civilization has a history of Being On A Mission of compelling entire cultures to Just Say Yes.[II] Perhaps it's true that *all* civilizations have been on imperial missions, though some, apparently, were content with multicultural diversity so long as taxes were paid and nobody made too much trouble.[III] The West, however, does not care for multiculturalism. It has had a passion for uniformity. I think the early spread of empire Catholicism demonstrates this Western tendency, from the early fight of the "orthodox" against all Christian "heretics," to the Crusades, to the suppression of the Albigensians, to the "ethnic cleansing" of Moors and Jews in Spain, to the Thirty Years War, to witch burning, to the "ethnic cleansing" of American Indians, to Hitler's Final Solution. I do not, however, mean to lay all this at the feet of the Catholic Church. In fact, I have seen in my own life that the richer heritage of institutional Catholicism (particularly the women's orders) produces far more sensitivity toward cultural variation than is the case among most Protestants. Protestants simply refocused Catholic uniformity into smaller and smaller flashlights, with narrower and narrower beams. The universal fear of God became, through doctrinal exactness, a laser tool for interrogating "pagan" error.

II. "Now the peoples of all the great civilizations everywhere have been prone to interpret their own symbolic figures literally, and so to regard themselves as favored in a special way, in direct contact with the Absolute. Even the polytheistic Greeks and Romans, Hindus and Chinese, all of whom were able to view the gods and customs of others sympathetically, thought of their own as supreme or, at the very least, superior; and among the monotheistic Jews, Christians, and Mohammedans, of course, the gods of others are regarded as no gods at all, but devils, and their worshippers are godless." So says Joseph Campbell on page 8 of his *Myths to Live By*.

III. While I have a kind of instinctive sympathy for the underdog, from the Jews in Europe through World War II to the Palestinians currently under brutal and humiliating occupation by Israel, this sympathy is tempered (see, for instance, "Al Qa'ida's Strategic Alliance," chapter 5 in Seth Jones' in *The Graveyard of Empires: America's War in Afghanistan*) by the realization that revolt against domination, when conducted under the ideological umbrella of theocratic conceptions or ethnic exclusions, can and does lead to horrific outcomes. Exhaustion may temporarily dissipate the energy of hate, but only love, repentance, acceptance, and reconciliation can undo the Spenglerian vicious cycle.

Science is, to some extent, the Inquisition's intellectual derivative—interrogating Nature to make her relinquish her stubborn secrets.

This drive for uniformity, needless to say, has not been confined to religious imperialism. The ancient Romans were aggressively imperial before Christianity existed, and our political heritage is only partly due to the Christian passion for uniformity—though the Religious Right constitutes a large hunk of righteous energy within imperial America. If I were to use conventional religious language, I could say the core energy within American imperialism is corporate and military and therefore "pagan." But this constitutes gross misuse of the term. "Pagan," of course, when thundered from the pulpit, means something is irreligious, worldly, false, corrupt, and probably evil. In reality, "pagan" is "peasant's" twin. Both words—peasant and pagan—derive from the Latin *pagus*, meaning "from the country" or a country locale. And while at first glance the etymology of "pagan" may seem either mildly interesting or purely irrelevant, it is in fact enormously revealing of a bias against rural life lodged in one of our most threatening and dangerous epithets. Urban Christians in Rome, on the fourth-century cusp of their merging with the Empire responsible for the murder of their founder, called their enemies "pagan" because their absorption into Empire prevented them from recognizing that the core enemy of the beloved community, of a more fully realized or articulated kingdom of God, was not the "pagan" but the *civilized*. Civilization killed Jesus. But the Church, in its merger with Empire, essentially abandoned its hopes and struggles in behalf of the kingdom of God in favor of a global mission aimed at converting the entire world to the universal and uniform doctrines of the True Faith, of which it claimed to be in sole possession. So began the inquisition of all false conviction. Civilization killed Jesus, but, as Christianity merged with civilization, "pagan" became a Christian scapegoat term whose function it was to deflect attention from the murderous propensities of civility. Its use and energy persist to this day. When the preacher reaches into his hat and pulls out a "pagan," so the politician reaches into his hat and pulls out a "terrorist." Like "pagan," "terrorist" works as an ethical filter preventing us from identifying with the victims of either "civilized" or "Christian" assault. How did we get ourselves into this sort of global psychodynamic pickle?

Here's where I put the finger primarily on civilization. All of my reading suggests it was male warrior energy—men with weapons and willing to use them—that coerced the precivilized agrarian village into becoming an expropriated peasantry. Here is the historic template for our situation and predicament. This dynamic of warrior aristocrat and expropriated peasant lies at the core of all civilizations, explicitly and openly so with preindustrial civilization. Industrial civilization no longer needed peasants, however, and therefore enforced their liquidation. This was true in England with the onset and spread of the modern Industrial Revolution, it was true in the Soviet Union under Stalin, and it was true in the United States—although here it was a slow and methodical garroting rather than an immediate and brutal decapitation. Agribusiness is *civilized* agriculture—an "agriculture" minus the human vitality of those who live on and work the land. Civilized bias in our most deeply institutionalized outlook—the language of "civility," the language of religious conviction— enabled a slide into Global Mission, a mission with many heads but linked in pervasive disregard for the rural, the agricultural, and the "pagan." With the liquidation of the peasantry, folk culture was thinned into a populist wraith even as the commercialization of new technologies (radio, movies, television, mass magazines, professional sports, etc.) enabled civilized substitutes for indigenous culture to emerge and be grabbed onto. It is this cultural weakening, in my estimation, what we might also call the ontological thinning of culture, that accounts for the fatal weakness of working-class unions—an elusive, uncomprehending drift from folk consciousness toward identification with national symbols, with the flag, with imperial impulse and militaristic pride. "Democrats for Reagan." (Not that Lyndon Johnson served the working class well. If Johnson was a "liberal," his mission to "bring home the coonskin" from Vietnam is reason enough to decline the liberal label. And Jonathan Schell's "The Fifty-Year War," in the November 30, 2009, issue of *The Nation*, with his warning to Barack Obama regarding Afghanistan vis-à-vis the lessons of Vietnam, once again underscores how "liberals" can't seem to resist the same macho tendencies that so captivate right-wing "conservatives.")

In principle, the Green Party—neither "liberal" nor "conservative," standing for (I quote its "four pillars") Ecological Wisdom, Social Justice, Grassroots Democracy, and Nonviolence—is the party of the postcivilized Daughter. *Post*civilized I say, and as such the Green Party's very existence contains prophetic impact. Just as the women's movement on a global scale signifies the beginning of the end of male warrior energy as the core principle of our collective organization, so the emergence of the Green Party points to cultural reconfigurations ahead.

Civilization killed Jesus and civilization wedded to monotheistic religions is killing the world. The male warrior energy that congealed into an aristocracy by enslaving the farmers in the precivilized agrarian village has been the core energy of all subsequent civilizations. That energy globalized and "democratized" is meeting its terminus. It is openly unsustainable, both culturally and ecologically. Civilization globalized is reaching the stage of collapse precisely because it is inherently brutal and predatory, and its "democratic" globalization now provides empirical proof of its unsustainability. To the extent that we can grasp these dynamics and absorb their transformative power is the extent to which we can get through this transition with a minimum of death, mayhem, and destruction. Sometimes I call this transformation "repentance," but don't get stuck or thwarted by a word. What matters is that we drop the filters that enable and sustain our acquiescence as we realize that safety and sanity do not depend on empire but, rather, on this spiritual transformation-in-progress. A variety of factors guarantees that transformational speed is going to intensify. The economy will of necessity be re-embedded in society, and civilization (with radically pruned "traumatic institutions") will be absorbed into culture. As Lewis Mumford said, in his final words in *The Pentagon of Power*, "But for those of us who have thrown off the myth of the machine, the next move is ours: for the gates of the technocratic prison will open automatically, despite their rusty ancient hinges, as soon as we choose to walk out."[3]

NOTES

1. Klein, "Trial," 10.
2. Parenti, "Empire," 28, 30.
3. Mumford, *Pentagon*, 435.

8

An Induced Absence of Discernment

IN 1980, ORBIS BOOKS published *Marxism: An American Christian Perspective* by Arthur McGovern. Oddly enough, the name "Ivan Illich" does not appear in the Index, despite the books written by Illich in the 1970s. But, then, neither does the word "civilization" appear in the Index, though that's less of a surprise, for neither Marxism nor Christianity has been particularly noted for its critique of civilization. What makes this puzzling in McGovern's *Marxism* is that one of his topics is liberation theology. How it's possible to truly explicate that subject, especially from within a Christian perspective, without constant reference to the contradiction and tension between civilizational governing structures and the deeply grounded ethical requirements of the kingdom of God, is bewildering.

In his second chapter ("Marxism: Its Development since Marx"), McGovern deals briefly with two thinkers from the Frankfurt School, Herbert Marcuse and Jurgen Habermas. He calls them "philosophers of the New Left." Marcuse, he says, insists we "need freedom *from* economy, freedom from politics, and freedom from the 'false needs' created by our present consumer society."[1] Habermas, McGovern says, asserts that the "economic base is itself now a function of government activity, taken up into the superstructure."[2] On its face, this seems a critique much like Ivan Illich's and an analysis amenable to a kingdom of God versus civilization explication.

Now it might be that "superstructure" can be construed as an equivalent term for "civilization." If so, the gist of the phrase "taken up into the superstructure" suggests that in the preindustrial past those who embodied the "economic base" (i.e., peasants and handicraft workers in particular) were culturally distinct from the "superstructure," not exactly part of it, not yet "taken up." They were, we might say, separate from and beneath it. To some large extent they held the superstructure up by their expropriated labor and taxed production.

That's not a terribly tough concept to get across. People pretty much get it. There were peasants and there were aristocrats, and the latter ran the show. The latter taxed the former and lived off the producers' "surplus." Those who lived with a degree of luxury, with servants, retainers, and soldiers, were the aristocrats. Theirs was the kind of life that embodied civilized values, whatever was supposedly enduring in culture and art. Aristocratic lives and princely actions were culturally representative of civilization, the vanguard and template of civility.

People also seem to get it that, with industrialization, the folk culture of preindustrial subsistence dried up, was in some cases deliberately crushed, and that people through industrialization were increasingly caught up in commercial and bureaucratic organization, relying on purchased commodities, working in ways far more rationally regimented and institutionally controlling than their ancestors had. Where the ancestors had been impounded as a distinctly lesser class—although a class fully capable of economic self-maintenance—the new industrial proletariat was, as a class, far less ecologically grounded or culturally adept. A commercially produced "popular" culture steadily replaced an atrophied folk culture.

Whenever I get a chance, I hop on my hobbyhorse and gallop into these issues. Like your ordinary religious proselytizer, I have learned to slip a "message" under the door, and it may be that the ho-hum response I typically get is due more to my crude exposition and inept enthusiasm than to the subject proffered. *Caveat emptor.* No solicitation allowed. In general, it appears that people do not like to have the word "civilization" presented in a negative light. People who are more patient will usually hear me out, but then (see the last section of chapter 8, "Kings as Prime Movers," in Lewis Mumford's *The Myth of the Machine*) they will tell me that "civilization" has another, truer, finer meaning, a meaning rich in curiosity, kindness, inventiveness, tolerance, and love; and, although it probably cannot be denied that there has been a negative side to "civilization," a shadow and somewhat more brutal side, this humane, artistic, and spiritual side is the Real McCoy, the real thing, the side that truly matters. Almost invariably I leave such conversations feeling that I've hardly made an impression, that "civilization," like the Phoenix, just keeps rising out of its own ashes, that it is, like God, eternal, and also, like God, the embodiment of the Good. Like Ronald Reagan, "civilization" is made of Teflon, and nothing unsavory sticks to its image.

In this vein, I'd like to talk about *The Challenges of Ivan Illich*, a "collective reflection" on the person, life, and thought of Ivan Illich, a book edited by Lee Hoinacki and Carl Mitcham. Illich was born in 1926, in or near what's now Croatia or perhaps Slovenia. Educated in Rome, he became an ordained Roman Catholic priest, worked in the early 1950s in a largely Puerto Rican parish in New York City, went to Puerto Rico, started a Spanish-language center in Mexico, got into trouble with the church, removed himself from active priesthood, wrote books, including *Deschooling Society*, *Tools for Conviviality*, *Medical Nemesis*, and *Toward a History of Needs*—books that Arthur McGovern had no reference to in 1980. One risks foolishness by talking about the "core" of Illich's thought; but for our purposes here I will say that the core was the discovery of subsistence as a cultural form, and then the championing of that cultural form in relation to the monopolistic "caring" or "service" institutions within modern industrial society. That is, Illich's thought, in the books listed above, is very much germane to the civilization versus kingdom of God exploration.

Challenges contains nineteen contributions by some pretty trenchant intellectuals, including essays by the editors Hoinacki and Mitcham. Not one is fluffy or lightweight. In some, the terminology is daunting. All the writers were strongly influenced by the penetrating, tough thinking of Ivan Illich. All reveal fierce, coiled resistances to the hegemony of modern institutions, especially "caring" institutions. The word "civilization" does not appear in the Index of *Challenges*, just as it does not appear in *Marxism*.

Now in McGovern's book, there are five page listings for "Kingdom of God." (I found two more usages in text, so there actually are seven.) The first of the seven is in a tiny section called "Protestant Social Thought in the United States," and here, in a paragraph on Walter Rauschenbusch, we are told that Rauschenbusch "argued that the message of the Kingdom *was* the social gospel."[3] There's a reference on page 110 to Vatican II. References on pages 189, 191, 192, and 196 are associated with liberation theology. And the final reference, on page 321, I will simply quote: "Any hope or plan for a new social order had to contain some utopian element. Christianity itself is filled with utopian hopes for the coming Kingdom of God."[4]

"Utopian" is something of a greased-pig word. It extrudes grease even as you try to wipe it off. It sweats grease, even in cold weather. (See Mumford's essay "Utopia, the City, and the Machine" in his collection *Interpretations and Forecasts: 1922–1972*.) The better word is "eutopian," and for this I recommend Mumford's The *Story of Utopias* or my *Green Politics Is Eutopian*. I think the kingdom of God, as advocated by Jesus in the first three Gospels especially, is far less a slippery sack of "utopian" hopes than it is a very serious and tough alternative organizing principle for social relations, an alternative to civilization. The kingdom of God, far from being elusively or ideationally "utopian," is exceedingly concrete. You-I-we are to be nonviolent servants unto each other. We are to live simple, compassionate, humble, truth-loving lives. We are not only to forgive our enemies but even love them. In this regard I would say that, in principle, the Green Party's Four Pillars—Ecological Wisdom, Social Justice, Grassroots Democracy, and Nonviolence—represent as close a political approximation to the kingdom of God as I've ever seen. That's not to say that anybody's "social gospel" exhausts or fully embodies the kingdom of God, only that such efforts as the Greens' are on the right path.

Although there are five Index references to "Jesus Christ" in Hoinacki and Mitcham's *Challenges*, there is no Index reference for "kingdom of God," just as there is none for "civilization." What does this tell us?

My friend David Kast (who knows Lee Hoinacki and who knew, less well, Ivan Illich) has shared with me a draft of a paper he's prepared for a conference on the condition of religion in the modern world. The image that most struck me in David's paper was this one: "We truly live *outside* the world. Think of us living high up on the fiftieth floor of a giant skyscraper, far from the earth below us, sustained by a constant infusion of stuff from outside because we cannot sustain ourselves as peoples any longer."[5] How did this happen? How did we get unsustainably on the fiftieth floor?

For Ivan Illich—this becomes explicit in *The Rivers North of the Future: The Testament of Ivan Illich as Told to David Cayley*—the wholesale institutional corruption of the modern world is a perversion of Christianity, a perversion of the Gospels. In particular, the "secularization" of the Samaritan story, the "this-worldliness" of the church, has "become the seed from which modern service organizations have grown." This is a perversion through institutionalization "which makes charity worldly and true faith obligatory."[6]

What I find missing in Illich is any sustained grappling with the huge historical momentum of what Mumford calls the "traumatic institutions" of civilization and what Toynbee calls civilization's "diseases." (Toynbee means by "diseases" Class and War. See his *Civilization on Trial*. And by "traumatic institutions" Mumford means the "centralization of political power, the separation of classes, the lifetime division of labor, the mechanization of production, the magnification of military power, the economic exploitation of the weak, and the universal introduction of slavery and forced labor for both industrial and military purposes."[7] This list is also in "Kings as Prime Movers," referenced earlier.) The belly button of the universe is apparently, for Illich, the church. I cannot help but get the impression that the church is, for him, so colossally important, so cosmically central, its "perversion" so significant, powerful, and pervasive, that little else matters historically. One can hardly overstate the importance of the church in Illich's constellation. It's not incidental that he felt so psychologically at home in the twelfth century, in a world where the church penetrated into virtually every aspect of social life.

But when the Roman church attached itself to the Roman Empire, its identity *merged* with empire, albeit initially as a minor and junior partner. Rome, as Empire, was then the Western embodiment of civilized traumatic institutions and diseases. One would not know any of this from reading Illich. Such an absence is, to me, astonishing. The only explanation I can come up with, as to why this is so, is that Illich was so absorbed, dedicated, and committed to an understanding of the church as the pulsating belly button of the universe—a doorway, an entrance, into a Holy Inside "the world" could not enter—that the etiology of civilization, with its traumas and diseases, shrank into historical and metaphysical insignificance, or, perhaps, the fourth-century marriage of Christianity and Empire, with the latter's unwitting one-flesh mystical susceptibility to salvation through marriage, resulted miraculously in a *holy* Roman Empire, with the Holy See as its heart and brain on Earth. Illich was fixated on the alleged mystical divinity of the church, its sacred-vessel nature, outside of which, apparently, there is no salvation. I believe one gets a glimpse into Illich's preoccupation when, in David Cayley's Introduction to *Rivers North of the Future*, Cayley tells us:

> The Samaritan's action, according to Illich, "prolongs the Incarnation" and would not be possible without the Incarnation; that is, it is a *revealed* possibility and not one that innately belongs to human beings. The Samaritan can dare to enter the no man's land that lies between cultures and separates him from the wounded one only because he is enacting God's love, the love revealed in Jesus.[8]

I find this spiritually bewildering. Instead of a brilliant folk tale told by Jesus, illustrative of spontaneous compassion across ethnic and religious boundaries, capable of being understood and internalized by anyone anywhere, the Samaritan story becomes dependent on a later theology that formalizes a doctrine of Incarnation as "enacting God's love, the love revealed in Jesus." You suddenly can't understand the story unless you've been prepared for it by subsequent theology! That means those who initially heard it couldn't understand it either. So it's something of a miracle they even bothered to write it down.

Well, I think it's possible to pull quite a few such passages out of *Rivers*, but here's one more from Cayley's Introduction:

> The proper vocation of the Church, [Illich] said, is not to instruct the world, guide its political and social orientation, or provide it with services. All these activities inevitably require the exercise of power and inevitably generate ideological division. The cross, for Illich, stands for the renunciation of power. It foreshadows a unity which is manifest in the world but never belongs to it, a unity always out of the reach of merely instrumental human purposes. The Church exists to discern and celebrate this mystery, rather than to accomplish some social or political end.[9]

The cross, I would respond, stands far less for the categorical renunciation of power than for the unmasking of civilization's mythological hypocrisy, and for what civilization actually *did* to Jesus for his articulation and embrace of the kingdom of God. If the nonviolent embracing love manifest in Jesus implies any renunciation, it is (at least in part) the renunciation of civilization as the principle governing social organization. It seems to me philosophically slippery and theologically dubious to say a generalized "renunciation of power" is what the cross stands for.[1] If Jesus on the cross represents some sort of cultural hinge, it is a hinge that enables us to identify with the victim. (In *Challenges*, go to Jean-Pierre Dupuy's "Detour and

---

1. For an exceptionally thorough and lucid alternative view, see *Binding the Strong Man: A Political Reading of Mark's Story of Jesus* by Ched Myers.

Sacrifice" for a useful contrast between Ivan Illich and Rene Girard.) With Illich, one wants to ask What power is to be renounced? Whose power? Power made manifest in what ways?

The power the church must renounce—both renounce and de-nounce—is the matrix of civilizational powers and principalities (including civilization's monopoly of "sacred violence") with which its identity is so entangled. In addition, the church has to abandon its religious impe-rialism, its *extra ecclesiam nulla salus*—"no salvation outside the church." Illich, it seems, evaded having to deal with these issues by simple avoid-ance. While there is in his writings an enormous amount of analysis showing how modern service institutions are perversions of the Gospel, there is nothing (that I know of) focusing on civilization as the template from which nearly all social institutions, including the exceedingly obvi-ous hierarchical structure of the Vatican, derive. It's almost as if Illich is to be compared to Margaret Thatcher, who reputedly said "There is no such thing as society." Perhaps for Illich there is no such thing as civilization.

I think this really has to do with Illich's lust for the church, perhaps even a "divine" Oedipus complex. The church is to be pure. It is to be powerless. Perhaps it is to be, like the Jesus ambiguously presented in the Gospel of John, not of this world. But if the church is (as it appears to be for Illich) the most important institution ever to appear on Earth, then it is obviously problematic to admit that civilization, institutionally older and structurally deeper, shaped the church in important ways different from, and even antithetical to, the spiritual energy and cultural intent of its founder, Jesus—if it is, in fact, intellectually honest and spiritually ap-propriate to call Jesus the church's "founder." Illich simply sidesteps this problem by carping about "this-worldly" perversion. But if the kingdom of God is *not* an alternative organizing principle in regard to civiliza-tion, if Spirit is *not* bubbling in our collective inner being, if the yeast of compassion and nonviolence is *not* steadily growing universally in the human soul, then our goose is cooked. As things fall apart, we may get to choose between global catastrophe and multinational aristocracy—even that's a stretch—but we can forget about the spiritual healing of traumatic (PTSD) institutions, the curing of civilization's diseases, or the realization of libertarian, ecological, democratic socialism.

If the divine is so spiritually aloof and withdrawn as Illich implies— "always out of the reach of merely instrumental human purposes"—

there's no way out of this mess. Doom is simply closing in on us.[II] But if the world blows to hell, it will be far less because of the "perversion" of Christian "caring" institutions, such as Illich alleged, than that Christians long ago abandoned their identity and affinity with the kingdom of God, as they constructed a multimillennial superstructure that insisted love for God demanded hatred of this world—the church as righteous spaceship loading for sandal-dusting lift-off. For it was as Otherworldly Transit that the church accepted its role in the Constantinian church/state division operative to this day. The state (civilization) gets to run the world, while the church gets to prepare otherworldly cargo for posthumous transport. The church may scold or chide the state on occasion, but the worldly *authority* of the state is supposedly God's will, and is not to be tampered with.

Now it is obviously true that infectious Gospel energy has had a *huge* influence in the creating and shaping of democratic consciousness in the Western world, an influence that has spread around the globe. So one could also say that a great many of the "caring" institutions Illich attacked for their "radical monopoly"—schooling, healthcare, "welfare" service institutions of all kinds—were the result of Gospel energy infecting civilized institutions in the direction of greater humanity and practical compassion, even as those institutions continued to carry an overbearing posture of political entitlement and cultural supremacy. That is, let's say, the impulse toward a "welfare state" can be profoundly ethical and compassionate even as the mind-set of bureaucrats and the institutional procedures of the welfare bureaucracy reflect uncritical projections of civilizational assumptions. Lacking a deeper spiritual understanding of the core predatory energy within civilizational momentum, and blinkered by an ethical condescension virtually obligatory because of inherited religious doctrine, it's no great mystery why so much of the "welfare" or "entitlement" process has been overburdened with bureaucratic waste and procedural red tape. If there is "perversion" here, it is in many ways less a perversion of Christian compassion seeking to "yeast" the cold, predatory institutions of civilization into universal humanitarian purpose than it is a perversion of long-standing Christian intellectuality—an induced

---

II. German theologian Dorothee Soelle, on page 139 of her *Against the Wind*, says "We need to go beyond giving aid in catastrophes and beyond charitable action, and trust the Holy Spirit who is not afraid of organization, structure, and theory, but uses them all for her purposes."

absence of discernment regarding the predatory nature of civilization's core organizational energy, its traumatic institutions and diseases, and the church's pathological schizophrenia regarding the "two kingdoms." That is, the church has had no critical appraisal of civilization, no sustained teaching in its regard (at least not sense the atrophy of the kingdom of God proclamation), by which to recognize in civilization not so much its God-given partner in "two-kingdom" governance as its spiritual antithesis. Lacking this discernment—remember, please, that the church/state division is built on this lack of discernment, built in fact to cloud and obstruct it—Christian compassion found nothing wrong in creating or enlarging "caring" institutions as the means became available within an industrial and (to some degree) democratic society. Was this a huge mistake? Not really. But even if it was a mistake, it was a secondary mistake, a subsidiary mistake, a mistake deriving from the Constantinian mistake, a weakness, a failure, a sin, the core of which was the ancient abandonment of the kingdom of God as the primary point of Jesus' message and the substitution of rigorous, orthodox, doctrinal certainty in otherworldly salvation. The real question is whether a fuller "yeasting" of civilization by Gospel-driven compassion can be achieved without also recovering the core insights within the kingdom of God proclamation, and whether such yeasting provokes or reveals a fundamental contradiction in dire need of resolution.

The church subsequently kissed and blessed and sanctified the state for so many generations that there is simply a huge void where there should be kingdom of God consciousness. Christianity saw itself, socially speaking, as applying, at best, a little Jesus tweaking to God's other arm. Lacking consciousness that the kingdom of God is a subversive digestive process, a spiritual fungus, intent on transforming civilization's diseases and traumatic institutions, who gets blamed for the current global mess? We are apparently still too mythologically blind to recognize or accept what Mumford and Toynbee tried to tell us. Instead, we will, like Ivan Illich, kick the crap out of the liberal do-gooders, those whose "misguided" compassion leads them to the "perversion" of institutionalized care. But nobody lays a glove on civilization. The word appears in nobody's Index.

Why, as David Kast asks, are we on the unsustainable fiftieth floor? Because, very early on, Christianity crawled into bed with civilization and betrayed the kingdom of God. So it's time for a Great Divorce, and, then, for a wonderful Truth and Reconciliation process. It's time to quit sucking the religious pacifier of spiritual powerlessness while waiting for God's eternal daycare bus. It's time to assert, whatever else Spirit may have in store for us, that *we live on Earth*, and it's time we actually learned to do so.

NOTES

1. McGovern, *Marxism*, 76.
2. McGovern, *Marxism*, 78.
3. McGovern, *Marxism*, 102.
4. McGovern, *Marxism*, 321.
5. Kast, "Hard," 4.
6. Cayley, *Rivers*, 179.
7. Mumford, *Myth*, 186.
8. Cayley, *Rivers*, 31.
9. Cayley, *Rivers*, 7.

9

A Theology of Cosmological Aspiration

THE APRIL 2, 2007, issue of *The Nation* has back-to-back book reviews, both interesting and engaging. The first review ("Made in USA" by Perry Anderson) deals with two books on former United Nations Secretary General Kofi Annan, and the second ("Take the Money and Run" by Steve Fraser) also meditates on two books, one on Andrew Carnegie and the other on Andrew Mellon. Both reviewers, in my estimation, using the books under consideration as handy springboards, take the opportunity to launch their own views on the subjects at hand. It is an indulgence I sympathize with, for reviews lacking critical response or argumentative dialogue can be pretty dry and boring, merely puff pieces. It's gotten to the point where, as a rule, I go first to book reviews in periodicals for the best and most insightful writing.

Perry Anderson has here written the most incisive thing I've ever read on the United Nations as a creature of the United States, while Steve Fraser touches into the underlying psychodynamics of power by which economic entities—and our lives—are organized. Carnegie and Mellon were, of course, Gilded Age robber barons. But let's permit Steve Fraser to establish the topic:

> When Carnegie and Mellon were coming of age, American society was still in the throes of creating a new structure of authority. Market society and capitalist industrialization carried with them a different foundation for the exercise of authority, one that no longer inhered in individuals (a feudal lord, for example) but rather in the alleged lawfulness of the system of exchange itself. It was the system that seemed natural, hence legitimate, and so commanded allegiance. No person, no matter his or her ostensible influence over daily life, could be held accountable for whatever relations of domination and inequality might result from the in-

exorable operations of the system. Carnegie and Mellon, whatever their vast differences in upbringing and personality (which these biographies make so vivid), were nonetheless, in their instinctive adherence to this way of looking at and behaving in the world, fundamentally alike.

Both men were creatures of the system.[1]

Here are what seem key phrases: "creating a new structure of authority" and "a different foundation for the exercise of authority." But I think we might also recognize in "the inexorable operation of the system" what Jurgen Habermas was driving at with his "economic base . . . taken up into the superstructure."

Well, Habermas aside, Fraser opens his review with reference to William Graham Sumner, whom he calls the "foremost exponent in America of Herbert Spencer's philosophy of social Darwinism." Lifting a passage from Sumner's 1883 *What Social Classes Owe to Each Other*, Fraser tells us that Sumner proclaimed "A free man in a free democracy has no duty whatever toward other men," and that "the next pernicious thing to vice is charity."[2] Anything but this hardheaded "realism" is only insidious sentimentality:

> As one can glean from Sumner's social Darwinian summa, this system was not merely a form of political economy; it aspired to be a cosmology. Its influence extended over the whole social order, infusing not only the political culture but higher education, the press, mainstream religion, even the manners and mores of society. Although Carnegie and Mellon were human, the system was not. It was inhuman, or perhaps more to the point, it was nonhuman, faceless. Inhuman suggests a normative indictment. And laissez-faire capitalism during the Gilded Age came in for plenty of that, condemned for its immorality and cruelty by victimized farmers and workers and smaller businessmen, by outraged journalists, novelists, preachers and even, now and then, a President or two. More inscrutable than the system's moral obtuseness, however, was its matter-of-fact implacability. Eerily impersonal, the economy was presumed to operate like some gigantic clockwork, according to its own ingenious mechanics, its designer unknown but beneficent. For captains of industry, not to mention their legions of admirers, this amounted to a faith in immaculate social evolution, free of human agency, absolved of all personal responsibility—a theology of economic deism. One either acted in conformity with the revealed laws of economic progress or else.

> Mellon and Carnegie did more than conform. They were ar-
> chitects of the new order. . . .[3]

I suppose we could therefore say, with or without irony, that Mellon and Carnegie were, as architects of the new order, theologians of economic deism. There is more to this than mere sardonic humor.

The linkage of authority to theology should come as no surprise. Theology may be, narrowly speaking, the study of God or an exploration into the nature of God; but certainly, for those of us raised Christian, any reference to God is also a reference to authority, even to Ultimate Authority. In this sense only God is truly sovereign. God's authority is so great and all-encompassing that all other sovereignty is derivative. This is a core principle within Western theology. We see this unmistakably in such language as King of kings, Prime Mover, or Supreme Being. We defer before authority and we are to defer before its derivatives. Darwinian capitalism is one such derivative before which we are to defer—a system so natural and legitimate that no person can be held accountable for any pattern of domination or blemish of inequality. Andrew Mellon, Treasury Secretary from 1921 until 1932, had a "dogged faith in the self correcting nature of 'the system,' absolving him of any obligation to act even in the face of its breakdown."[1] The breakdown in question for Mellon was the Great Depression and, as Fraser goes on to say, the "old order, now made defunct by the Depression, was supplanted by a new one that weighed in on the side of social security, the rights of labor, regulation of business and economic redistribution."[4]

It took another fifty years, up to the presidency of Ronald Reagan, for an explicit theology of economic deism to come back with unfettered

---

I. One cannot help but think of climate change in regard to this absolving of obligation to act in the face of breakdown. It is an enormous puzzle how the rich and powerful can continue to be so willfully oblivious to the long-term consequences of global warming, or how the political establishment does so stunningly little to address it. One possibility is, of course, sheer cynical indifference. But it's impossible to believe that explanation works for most people, for nearly everyone I've ever known (William Graham Sumner notwithstanding) has concern for the well-being of family and descendants. That really leaves only two major options—either a real conviction of imminent End Times or a dogged faith in the self-correcting nature of "the system." That is, the psychospirituality of civilizational hubris is apparently so deeply embedded in the operational mentality of the rich and powerful—but not only the rich and powerful—that only literal disintegration can break into its encapsulated self-assurance. I can think of no other adequate explanation.

power, this time marvelously entangled with a Christian Right eager for End Times. Since the world was soon coming to a close, what need was there for economic limitation or military restraint? Why worry about world ecology? Let's strip mine more coal, as James Watt urged, because Jesus is coming. Let's rip the tops off mountains. So began the prospect for a new American century.

The point I am dancing around here has to do with our psychocultural muddle regarding democracy and authority. While we all can make a grocery list of what constitutes authority in our lives, it may be possible to argue that all ultimate power is in the end sacred. But for our purposes here, however, I desire separate categories for secular and sacred. I would argue that the core of authoritative power lies in the realm of the secular, the fundamental force that shapes virtually all the institutions of our society—government, schools, hospitals, the economy, etc.—as well as the policies by which these institutions are guided, funded, and energized. But because such governance (in the broad sense) has a hard time both to conceal its abuses (ripping the tops off mountains) and to justify its inequalities (huge wealth inequities), it needs an overlay of sacred explication. We must be reasonably convinced that God wants things this way, that God has secret and mysterious purposes even if the facts on the ground, as it were, defy any thoughtful ethical rationale. The raw and ugly secular must be packed and packaged in the protective wrappings of the sacred, in the tissue of God's will. We must be convinced of our systemic religious superiority, and only God (or some derivative facsimile like the Constitution) has the eternal capital by which to ensure such brutal and risky investment.

It is no accident that *the* core electoral base within American economic deism is the Christian Right. Without such sacred protection, the secular Right's brazen empire hubris would be quickly blocked by democratic (and ecological) considerations. And that immediately raises the question of why the Left (despite the electoral success of Democrats in November 2006 and 2008) invariably projects less moral authority than the Right.[II] A related question is why the Right is still convention-

II. Jonathon Schell, in "The Fifty-Year War," an article in *The Nation* referenced in a previous essay, asks on page 22, regarding what appears to be Barack Obama's fatal repeat in Afghanistan of Lyndon Johnson's military escalation in Vietnam, "What is the source of this raw power, this right-wing veto over presidents, Congress and public opinion? The person who can answer these questions will have discovered one of the keys to a half-ally dressed in the semantic garb of "conservative" when essentially all its policies are the antithesis of conserving or conservation. In fact, the seeming absurdity of aligning the Right with "conservative" is the clue to the question of why the Left projects authority so poorly.

The Right is conservative in only one way: it thrusts itself forward as the embodiment of *traditional values*, and at the core of that assertion is its identification with the overriding Western cultural conception of God, the God who is the glowering protector of civilized transcendence, a God of male impatience and overwhelmingly wrathful power. Historically one sees this at its fullest social articulation when the Holy Roman Empire was at its height, when God the Father stood at the apex of social hierarchy, and all that fell below the Father were steps in a descending order ordained by God. It was, indeed, a sacred order. From the omnipotent God to the dynastic king to the lowest dirty peasant, sacred order prevailed. (So when Steve Fraser, in the last paragraph of his review, quotes George Baer, president of the Philadelphia and Reading Railroad, as saying "The rights and interests of the laboring men will be protected and cared for by the Christian men to whom God has given the control of the property rights of the country," we should not only be hearing a summing up of the worldview of America's new industrial autocracy, but also an updated articulation of traditional hierarchical values.[5] This is far less a "new structure of authority" than a reformulated, old—even ancient—assertion of authority.)

Christianity has broken denominationally into lots of pieces, and the more liberal of these denominations are in a fairly advanced state of theistic decomposition. Sacred hierarchy in those institutions is as soggy and saggy as a wet cardboard church. God is not what He used to be. The Son has been made hugely more human and existentially ethical by the scholarship of such people as Marcus Borg and John Dominic Crossan. And the Holy Spirit, thanks to people like Rosemary Radford Ruether, Elaine Pagels, Dorothee Soelle, and Joan Chittister, is in the process of removing Her male disguise and stepping forward in full radiant Femaleness. (When She has stepped fully forward, one of Her first acts will be the restoration of the repressed and buried Mother.) Against these revelations working their way into and through cultural forms stands the Christian

---

century of American history—and the forces that, even now, bear down on Obama as he considers what to do in Afghanistan." Schell's agonized question is perfectly apt, despite his excessively short time frame of a mere half-century.

Right, stridently denouncing all such revelation as the work of the Devil. The more theistically decomposed the Left becomes, the more strident and judgmental the Right convinces itself to be, and therefore the more relevant and revealing become these thoughts from Paul Tillich's *On the Boundary*:

> [M]y fundamental theological problem arose in applying the relation of the absolute, which is implied in the idea of God, to the relativity of human religion. Religious dogmatism, including that of Protestant orthodoxy and the most recent phase of what is called dialectical theology, comes into being when a historical religion is cloaked with the unconditional validity of the divine, as when a book, person, community, institution, or doctrine claims absolute authority and demands the submission of every other reality; for no other claim can exist beside the unconditioned claim of the divine. But that this claim can be grounded in a finite, historical reality is the root of all heteronomy and all demonism. The demonic is something finite and limited which has been invested with the status of the infinite.[6]

Christianity—or, perhaps we should more narrowly say, a certain large slice of Christianity on the Right—now claims this absolute authority, demanding the submission of every other reality, including every other religious or spiritual reality on a global scale. This kind of Christianity is, in Tillich's terminology, demonic. Christian imperialism is fueled by this demon. Underlying and undergirding this Christian demonism is the civilized inheritance Mumford and Toynbee warned us about—the traumatic institutions of bondage, violence, and inequality, the diseases of class and war.

Again we are back to what the late lay theologian William Stringfellow called the Constantinian Arrangement, that formal tipping point in the fourth century when the kingdom of God was headed for monastic retreat and the church became a spacecraft gathering souls for The Journey Home. The Christian Right, with its spacecraft heritage, has its mind Elsewhere, and it swats down, with might and main, everything that, in its view, corrupts the purity of that Elsewhere longing. Stringfellow says that with the Constantinian Arrangement,

> . . . signaled by the conversion of the emperor and the establishment of Christianity as the official religion of the Roman Empire, a comity between church and nation was sponsored that, in various

elaborations, still prevails in the twentieth century. The incidents that occasioned the Constantinian Arrangement, as such, are not as significant for contemporary Christians, or for either church or state today, as the ethos spawned and nourished by that comity and the mentality that has been engendered and indoctrinated by it over so long a time. It is, put plainly, an ethos that vests the existence of the church in the preservation of the political status quo. This inbreeds a mentality, affecting virtually all professed Christians, and most citizens whether Christian or not, which regards it as normative for the church's life to he so vested. And that has caused radical confusions in the relations of church and nation, church and state, church and regime. It has encouraged and countenanced stupid allegiance to political authority as if that were service to the church and, *a fortiori*, to God. Venerable though it be, this accommodation, and the way of conceiving of the juxta-position of church and political authority that it has inculcated for so very long, accounts more than anything else for the profound secularization of the church in the West and for the inception of Christendom as the worldly embellishment of Christianity.[7]

Here is the proper response to Ivan Illich's hand-wringing about secu-larization; it is not nearly so much a question of the perversion of the Samaritan story as it is and has been allegiance to political authority, an ethos spawned and nourished, created and sustained by the Constantinian Arrangement, although I am less inclined to say "profound secularization of the church," as Stringfellow does, than profound etherealization.

Meanwhile, as the Right waits for the End to arrive, it must see to the submission of every other reality. Will this help set the stage for End Times? Of course. Believing Christians will do their part, includ-ing support for politicians who pander to the Right, to help prepare the conditions for the supposed fulfillment of Revelation. But if this kind of Christianity is demonic, then who or what is its God? Is it the Devil, the father of misrepresentations and lies? Such questions begin to reveal the alarming ethical abyss between Gospel and Myth, between a theological decomposition that has begun to intuit Spirit in deep inner recesses and an externalized and transcendent theological triumphalism preparing for rapture in an inexpressibly glorious Elsewhere.

So when will we arrive at a new structure of authority? Only, it seems, when civilizational hubris and religious triumphalism are finally crushed by the forces, the contradictions, inherent in their own internal structures, when those internal contradictions are either recognized and repented of or carried out to their logical catastrophic conclusion. Hubris and triumphalism are in many ways astonishingly blind. Their literalistic captivity by what appears to them to be the unconditional validity of the divine makes them stupid and brutal. But where Christianity of the Right has only metaphysical fear and biblical literalism by which to spread its brand of authority, civilization has instruments of coercion and destruction beyond all historical comparison. If spiritual discernment in a political mode will not be able to democratically rein in this globalized, rampant hubris, it will hopefully be sufficiently purged, purified, and prepared to govern humanely and ecologically (libertarian, democratic, ecological socialism) once civilizational hubris has crashed and burned.

Our core task is the deepening and spreading of spiritual discernment, both a dovish grasp of what the kingdom of God meant and still means, and a wise-as-serpents understanding of the killer robot living in the Trojan horse called civilization. The growth of such discernment may well be our only hope for eluding either catastrophe or aristocratic restoration, or both in their own perverse measure.

NOTES

1. Fraser, "Take," 32.
2. Fraser, "Take," 30.
3. Fraser, "Take," 32.
4. Fraser, "Take," 35, 36.
5. Fraser, "Take," 36.
6. Tillich, *On*, 40.
7. Stringfellow, *Keeper*, 259.

10

The Underlying Religion of Civilization

T HE QUESTION OF AUTHORITY keeps returning. In the long term, power derives from authority or settles into place on the basis of authority, as in institutions of governance. Such power, including the power to destroy and kill, has legal sanction. (If you doubt this, just listen to our political leaders as they justify current military interventions in Iraq and Afghanistan.) Although there are varieties of power, including the power of the guy with a knife who might rob you in an alley, legitimate power can rob you with legal sanction—like the IRS, the company that owns your credit card, the no-bid "defense" contractor, the Wall Street firms that implode the entire economy and whose CEOs are so guilt-ridden they jump happily from skyscrapers wearing golden parachutes, or the Congress that deepens public debt to pay for military explosions and financialized implosions to the point where your unborn grandchildren will arrive saddled with fiduciary obligations they may or may not be able to discharge in their entire lifetimes.

For power to be sustained over the long haul, it must become legitimate authority. At some level, ultimately, we have to believe in or at least willingly defer to the power that robes itself in legitimizing authority. We do this all the time—when we pay the checkout girl at the supermarket, when we apply for a driver's license, when our child gets on the school bus, when we salute the flag or sing the Star-Spangled Banner, when we recite a religious creed. Our lives are saturated with patterns of deference to authority. We may be angry or resentful toward that authority, but we continue to defer to it.

Much of the hand-wringing regarding the deterioration of Western culture, at least on the Right or "conservative" side, is given to an analysis that bemoans the breakdown of legitimate authority even as, in my estimation, we are living in a period when inherited "legitimate" authority is crumbling under the weight of its accrued obsolescence and inherent contradictions. That is, a great deal of "social breakdown" derives from the impact of novel capitalist economies on traditional cultural forms; but the Right, in reflexive defense of capitalism, claims breakdown is caused by an abandonment of "values." Such an assertion works like a stun gun; it immobilizes the intellect as it substitutes abstraction for analysis, myth for history. The rhetoric of "values" appears plausible, but it has little if any traction when it comes to actual analysis. Its relevance is supposedly tied to the conventional image of God. That is precisely why the concept has had such extensive usage by the Right. Its function in behalf of moral outrage is as inexhaustible as it devoid of substance.

I think it safe to say that what we now call "the Western world" was shaped, from top to bottom, by the steady spread of the Holy Roman Empire, a congealed blend of civilizational emperor worship and mono-theistic God worship, steadily extinguishing or repressing all indigenous spiritualities in the process, whether European or American. If the idea was to "civilize" the entire world, or to "Christianize" it, the processes were interdependent and overlapping. The missionary with the cross walked right behind the soldier with a sword. Native American cultures were overpowered, both for religious and civilizational reasons, as soon as it was physically possible to overpower them. From 1800 to 1900, roughly, the entire continental "United States" was conquered, rescued from its status as red savage wilderness and liberated into white Christian civility, even as black plantation labor was emancipated from outright legal servitude into quasi-legal Jim Crow destitution, and brown subsistence farming was forced south of the Rio Grande. The *authority* to do this, to pull off this monumental invasion, suppression, and massive theft, rested both in the civilizing and Christianizing impulses. They were the strong metaphysical horses pulling the covered wagon of Progress across the wild prairie.

Internal to both impulses was a powerful antirural bias. With civi-lization one hardly needs to explain the assertion, for civilization is by definition the supremacy of aristocratic urbanity over against which the rustic countryside is merely the locale for material provisioning and a little rough adventure. Civilization is an empty term without the empire hubris of the city. In Rome, by the fourth century C.E., the antithesis to the Christian was already identified as the pagan, and, as we have seen, *pagus* is the countryside or country person—or, as Oswald Spengler puts it, the "young Church took the urban Western tendency decisively, so decisively that later it could describe the remaining heathen as '*pagani*,' country-folk."[1] And, a century later, the pre-eminent Christian ideal, now fused with empire, becomes explicit as the *City* of God.

I would argue that Jesus and his teachings are not altogether "Christian" even though later theology and church structure pretty rigidly defined what "Christian" is and is not, irrespective of Jesus and his "kingdom" proclamation. So when I align Christianity with civilization—or, rather, when I point to their long-standing political alignment—I am in no way attacking Jesus, the Gospels, or the kingdom of God but, rather, their antithesis, which is civilized Christianity or (it amounts to the same thing) Christianized civility. Authority is lodged in these latter constructs, in the metaphysical team of Civilization and Christianity pulling a fifty-bottom Plow of Development across the savage prairie, transforming wilderness into agribusiness, displacing Indian villages and wandering herds of bison for bovine feedlots and Wal-Mart parking lots.

All manner of folks can (and do) talk about "breakdown," but most of this talk only piddles with or even contributes to the muddle. That is, the explicit congealing of civilization and Christianity, since at least the early fourth century C.E., has resulted, with various ups and downs, in Christendom, nation-states, global conquest and colonialism, the industrial revolution, and massive urbanization. As this congealing has intensified its technological complexity simultaneously with its globalization, traditional noncivilized cultures and natural ecological configurations have been severely damaged, and "breakdown" comes in a vast array of possibilities, from rampant alcoholism to climate change. The glorious City of God is ramifying as the dystopian City of Man. It could be said that terrorism has become the single biggest poster child of "breakdown" hysteria, if we mean by hysteria a psychopolitical formula for the avoidance of real issues and the capacity to inflate effects into causes. Terrorism is apparently what the God of civilization craves to see destroyed, with some considerable help from the Marines—who will, incidentally, instill some discipline into your listless, wayward, or troubled son or daughter as they learn to be (*semper fidelis*) always faithful.

Our subject is authority. I would argue that it is precisely the inherited, traditional authority within our Western institutions, religiously sacrosanct and even politically holy, that has reached the level of hegemonic power (through globalized technology or technological globalization) by which its internal falsity and unacknowledged contradictions are now revealing their very undivine and very unsustainable characteristics—or, as Paul Tillich might say, their demonic characteristics. This authority is now cracking up. The attempt to *call us back* to the righteousness of earlier authority, to *return us* to "civilized values" or to "traditional faith," is simply not credible. But I want to be clear. There is a pocket of "civilized values" that really does embrace understanding and nonviolence, just as the Gospel continues (in tiny slivers and fragments) to be read from the pulpit. These are real where and when they occur, and they are to be honored. But they are small, strong threads in a massive garment that otherwise is falling apart.

The real test of our spiritual mettle in the coming breakdown depends on the extent to which Gospel yeast has or has not adequately leavened our spirits, for as our spirits are (or are not) leavened by the spiritual ethos of stewardship and servanthood, so that leavening (or its absence) is directly and proportionately reflected in our culture, in our social and political arrangements, and in our ecological behavior. Gospel's function is to create a new human ethos and cultural spirit, with corresponding sensitivities and complementary behaviors, and it cannot help but undermine pre-existing structures of authority, especially as those pre-existing structures are based on exploitation and coercion, traumatic institutions, and diseases of class and war. The older certainties of authority have, of course, been breaking down. The religious Right represents a "values" holdout and, as is obvious since the presidency of Ronald Reagan in particular, the Right aligns itself eagerly and enthusiastically with an aggressive empire politics cloaked in *moral* values, so that military interventions, for instance, are presented as ferociously righteous.

One could say the great failure of the Left is its inability to publicly project an alternative vision, a wiser ethos. But there are various reasons for this failure. First, the Left, where it has "come to power," has either done so by violence (as in the Soviet Union, China, and Cuba) or it has made major accommodations with capitalist economics and pre-existing patterns of state violence (as in France and England). Second, the collapse of traditional authority, while it can feel liberating, can also be deeply demoralizing. What we were taught to trust has proven itself untrustworthy, and we feel spiritually adrift. (And, often, revolutionary politics has aligned itself closely with anticlerical sentiments, thus discrediting previous order—both secular and religious—simultaneously. Filling that void is intellectually difficult and spiritually strenuous, to put it mildly.) Third, judgmental condemnation coming from the Right causes those with fresh and tender insight to refrain from casting pearls before swine, knowing that such vulnerable insight is likely to be trampled by the heavy feet of convention and orthodoxy. Fourth, even where Gospel insight is strong and vigorous, the major media and the major political venues are not exactly embracing of this message, for it is antithetical to "realism" and *Realpolitik*. Fifth, the dominant belief-system of the people has been shaped by the metaphysics and ideology of traditional authority, of Civilization and Christianity in golden harness, and to articulate a Green Gospel message of radical servanthood and radical stewardship, as a possible political springboard for the kingdom of God, is to cause jaws to drop. Such gymnastic articulations are so contrary to inherited messages of individualistic self-entitlement and moralistic powerlessness that they simply cannot be understood without, in some dimension, plunging the listener into a crisis of authority identity and spiritual credibility— the gymnast versus the catatonic, or the gymnast urging the catatonic to dance. (Luke 7:31–32.) Underlying all this in the Western world is the ancient atrophy of the kingdom of God as a concept of persistent articulation and, correspondingly, the hypertrophy of the Constantinian Arrangement whereby the church made its long-standing (and seemingly permanent) accommodation with imperial power, thus legitimizing that power (including its violence), and reducing the church to an otherworldly salvation agency. To wake up to the kingdom of God is to recover from a seventeen-hundred year spiritual paralysis and intellectual coma.

The People's Party of the late nineteenth century almost pulled off that political awakening, at least up to a certain point, because the great bulk of small farmers, in desperate financial straights, had never been fully saturated with urbane civility or theological rationalizations. They were emotionally closer to their peasant forebears; they had not yet been taught that cooperatives are evil or that God hates socialism. They may have been prone to what we now call fundamentalism, but the populist brand of "fundamentalism" was certainly not locked into a cynical electoral agenda cunningly manipulated by the Right. (See *The Populist Moment* by Lawrence Goodwyn.) Well, having evoked Goodwyn, even parenthetically, let's just lift a passage from his book:

> Twentieth-century people, reduced to the sobering knowledge that theirs, politically, is the least creative century of the last three,

take refuge in private modes of escape and expression, found largely through the pursuit and consumption of products. The corresponding decline in the vitality of public life verifies the constraints of modern political thought. "The people," though full of anxiety, do not know what to do politically to make their society less authoritarian. Language is the instrument of thought, and it has proven difficult for people to think about democracy while employing hierarchical terminology. On the available evidence, twentieth-century people around the globe are paying a high price for their submission to the hierarchical languages of political analysis that have grown out of the visions of Adam Smith and Karl Marx. The problem that will doubtless interest future historians is not so much the presence, in the twentieth century, of mass political alienation, but the passivity with which the citizenry accepted that condition. It may well become known as the century of sophisticated deference.[2]

Well, in terms of "deference" and "submission," we might say the twentieth century has continued cheerfully into the twenty-first, intensified by the implosion of "Karl Marx" and the manic expansion of "Adam Smith," intensified by the evermore alarming erosion of folk culture forms and the evermore advanced layering of technological and organizational substitutes. But this is exactly what the industrial revolution has enabled—the destruction of that social class from which Jesus arose (the peasantry), the class closest in cultural and ecological comprehension to the teachings of radical servanthood and radical stewardship. I think it possible to see the People's Party in precisely this manner—the desperate political clarity of an agrarian class facing extinction. That is, the People's Party represented the last gasp of the Jeffersonian "peasantry" in America, the political end of the Neolithic.

Yet it is not new or novel to say that the two priceless blessings arising from this hegemonic globalizing process (unintended as they may be) are racial and sexual equality. Although "equality" may not end up being the term of choice or preference (for it has an ambience of abstract mathematics, of quantitative equivalence, perhaps even of bland uniformity), it has its usefulness, and it has useful implications even as a concept of equivalence. For as Euro-American colonialism was racist and unequal—and it obviously was—a nonracist and "equal" relationship therefore implies less the rise of "the colored" to the level of "the whites" (itself a racist notion containing the implied supremacy of Western civilized and religious institutions) than the depression of inflated "white" self-regard and the recognition of desirable attributes within the varied cultures of "the colored." Equality is a concept of limited value if it does not imply and embrace richer understanding, acceptance, and reconciliation. There may be different ways of being human, but all those ways *are* human. And if it's true that every culture has something that's special or even superior, it would be pathetic to assert that violence is therefore the requisite means by which that superior specialty is to be forcibly spread and shared.

"Racism" has much more buried in its righteous body than mere ethnic favoritism or skin-color preference. Its *authority* is heavily informed by metaphysical supremacy in both a religious and civilizational sense.[1] Plantation slavery and the suppression of native cultures were only superficially about skin color; they overwhelmingly had to do with notions of "primitivism" and "savagery," states of being that were to be righteously supplanted by religious and civilizational forms of superiority. The pagan could be both exploited and suppressed; and if there was ambiguity, morally speaking, about exploitation, there was little ambiguity about suppression.

Even deeper in many ways is the liberation of women. Arthur Gish, in his *Hebron Journal*, says "There is only one basic religion in the world," and that is "faith in the saving power of violence." He says the "religion of redemptive violence is rooted in the Babylonian creation myth, in which the universe is created out of the parts of the goddess Tiamat's dismembered body." Although Gish immediately asserts that "The creation stories in the Jewish, Christian, and Muslim Scriptures . . . affirm that the universe was created by a good God and is basically good," and that "Redemption is possible without more violence," I think we have to ask what it might mean for the "religion of redemptive violence" to be "rooted in" the dismembered body of the goddess Tiamat.[3]

Following the schema of Mother, Father, Son, and Daughter, it's possible to at least ask whether this Babylonian myth does not reveal, or at least hint at, the brutal suppression of the precivilized agrarian village whose spirituality (and politics?) derived from the all-embracing Mother. What Arthur Gish doesn't say is that *the story of the dismembered female*

I. George L. Mosse's 1978 book, *Toward the Final Solution: A History of European Racism*, contains a great deal that is fully applicable in regard to contemporary American right-wing "populism," both in *how* it emerges and *why*, although Muslims are now assigned the moral depravity previously attributed to Jews.

stands at the very dawn of civilization, at that precise moment when armed male coercion violently extorts agricultural abundance from the agrarian village for the pleasure of the king in his city—the advent of the Father's reign, the ascendancy of hegemonic male domination. The "religion of redemptive violence" is *the real underlying religion of civilization,* and it begins with the violent dismemberment of Tiamat's body, that is, with the economic, cultural, and spiritual dismemberment of the precivilized agrarian village.

This system of redemptive violence, corruptingly and perversely "democratized" through the (largely misunderstood) spiritual energy of the Son (as perverted by the Constantinian Arrangement), is now globalized, its inherent contradictions erupting through layers of sanctifying theologies and sanctimonious rationalizations, its "blowback" bursting forth in multiple toxic dimensions. Libertarian democratic ecological socialism, under the sheltering arms of the Daughter's spiritual incarnation, signals the end of religion as redemptive violence, for it spirals us back to the dismembered village even as our spiritual awareness has been (and continues to be) purified by the subtle workings of kingdom of God ethics—servanthood and stewardship.

How does one talk about "authority" in regard to the new, unfolding sensibility? This new authority is radically unlike the prevailing authority, which has been rooted in economic advantage-taking and violent retaliation. To get to this new, gentle authority we have to embrace ethically humble servanthood and reverent stewardship, hold them in our hearts, as we wait for the old authority to die its blind dinosaur death. And although it *is* possible to live now within this fuller comprehension, it does not yet have anything resembling adequate spiritual inclusion or cultural recognition. Its political traction is growing, but it is not yet of sufficient consequence.

NOTES

1. Spengler, *Decline*, 291.
2. Goodwyn, *Populist*, 318.
3. Gish, *Hebron*, 263.

11

Our Settled Resignation

PROFESSOR ANDREW BACEVICH, IN the April 23, 2007, issue of *The Nation*, has a review in which he uses five books on (among other things) presidential power to explore American imperial impulses. In the process, he gives as lucid a reason as I've ever seen for the failure of the Democrats to initiate impeachment proceedings against Bush and Cheney: "The aim of the party out of power is not to cut the presidency down to size"—whatever size that may be—"but to seize it, not to reduce the prerogatives of the executive branch but to regain them."[1] That's not only a plausible insight, it also suggests that party-affiliated ideological entities are far less interested in the constitutional separation of powers than in gaining maximum advantage for the party as a whole, even as this maximum advantage steadily increases the accrued and accruing power of the executive branch, which in turn makes capturing the presidency by far the most important prize.

Somewhere in the late 1990s, in a thrift store, I found Amaury de Riencourt's *The Coming Caesars*. I'd never heard of the man or the book. But I was fascinated (the title is a compact summation of the book's prophetic theme) even as I quickly concluded de Riencourt was, at least in one dimension of his analysis, seriously misrepresenting the democratic impulse. In the opening paragraph of his Introduction, de Riencourt says it is

> . . . expanding democracy [that] leads unintentionally to imperialism and that imperialism inevitably ends in destroying the republican institutions of earlier days; further, that the greater the social equality, the dimmer the prospects of liberty, and that as society becomes more equalitarian, it tends increasingly to concentrate absolute power in the hands of one single man.[2]

What we've seen, however, even as the prerogatives of the executive branch have become more flagrantly imperial, is precisely the opposite trend from the one de Riencourt suggests. Instead of greater social equality, at least as measured by income, we've had increasingly less equality, sharply so.[1] Perhaps de Riencourt has a private definition of democracy; but he goes on to compare and contrast the shift from republic to empire in ancient Rome and the corresponding power shift going on in America since at least the Civil War. This comparing and contrasting was illuminating because so much of de Riencourt's analysis parallels the destruction of small-farm communities, the demographic bloating of cities and suburbs, and the atrophy of rooted local culture in favor of abstracted (but powerful) forms of civilized identity, including psychological association with corporate brand names. "Democracy" seems to be the label de Riencourt sticks onto enforced "proletarian," industrial, commercial, disoriented rootlessness, even as he repeatedly shows the agents of Roman cultural breakdown to have been economic predation and political elitism, a combination of corporate (or aristocratic) agribusiness consolidation and empire militarism. That is, de Riencourt's explicit analysis shows the monstrous consolidation of oligarchic power in both ancient Rome and modern America, and yet he can somehow blame "expanding democracy" as the culprit leading to imperialism. That such a lucid analysis can lead to such a contrary conclusion is downright weird and perhaps even loony.

Now it may be true that demands for democracy and equality increase as traditional cultural forms atrophy or are broken; one can certainly make such an argument in explaining the extension of democracy in this country from white males to white females to all ethnic groups, although the welfare state, with its corresponding bureaucratic bundle of "entitlements," says far less about equality than it says about the dispersal of imperial largesse for purposes of public quiescence. But to say, as de Riencourt does, that democracy leads to imperialism is to blame those whose lives are most destabilized—those *victimized* by economic advantage-taking and military aggression—for *causing* the imperial decay of republican institutions. The concentration of power in the executive branch is a *consequence* of an insufficient and tepid democracy whose political options have been increasingly channeled by corporate money via corporate

1. As early as 1993, Kevin Phillips was already documenting the trend toward inequality in his *Boiling Point: Democrats, Republicans, and the Decline of Middle-Class Prosperity.*

media, as well as by the governmental framework set up by the Founders, a framework that obviously was a "democratized" form of British governance: the House of Commons became our House of Representatives, the House of Lords our Senate, and the King our President. The concentration of power in the presidency is only another form of power concentration comparable to CEOs in their corporate fiefdoms. In political terms, it is the creeping restoration of aristocratic prerogative. In social terms, it is the steady wreckage and disablement of the small-scale. That is, as commercial and corporate forces have undermined and wrecked folk identity, executive prerogative, both in a governmental and commercial sense, has no independent folk base to contend with, just as the working class in America never matured sufficiently to create a socialist political party. Lawrence Goodwyn goes quite deeply into this issue:

> Populist theory poses the central twentieth-century political question: can large government be democratic? The history of twentieth-century industrial societies indicates not—at least not within the prevailing conceptual limitations of traditional capitalism and traditional socialism. Unfortunately, the idea that workable small-unit democracy is possible within large-unit systems of economic production is alien to the shared presumptions of "progress" that unite capitalists and communists in a religious brotherhood. So much so that the very thought tends to give people a headache. Intellectual short-circuits crackle everywhere. The topic, therefore, is not one the young are encouraged to speculate about; such a possibility challenges our settled resignation and puts people ill at ease. It is simpler to sustain one's morale by teaching the young not to aspire too grandly for too much democracy.
>
> The conclusion is transparent: the intellectual range of modern industrial societies is quite narrow. One observes that this conclusion is avoided by participants in the mainstream of capitalist and socialist societies because, to do otherwise, in sophisticated circles, is not career oriented and, in unsophisticated circles, is unpatriotic.[3]

In other words, empire (at least in its oligarchic and industrial forms) crushes small-scale culture and produces an imperial "democracy" manipulated by money, sustained by advertising, and locked into immobility by mythological rhetoric. With the rise of the Christian Right, sophisticated careerism and unsophisticated patriotism have united to prove Amaury de Riencourt perversely correct; that is, we certainly see the emergence of

Caesar—that part is alarmingly true—even as de Riencourt's explanation for *why* it's true is hogwash.

We have empire because, given our spiritual imperialism, we are awash in the sins of arrogance, greed, and pride; and such countertendencies as have been mounted politically (like the People's Party or the contemporary Greens) have been crushed or simply marginalized. What we need, of course, is political "kingdom of God" governance heavily informed by an underlying spirituality with strong ethical convictions. That is, while I am predisposed to be a democrat, predisposed to democracy, I have also seen how horrific brutalities have been justified through nominally democratic procedures—say the war against Vietnam or the current wars against Iraq and Afghanistan.

People like Amaury de Riencourt point accusingly at political philosophers like John Locke for promoting an extreme individualism in which "persons are separate mental substances without other relations than those of human reason." Locke, says de Riencourt, "hammered the last nail in the coffin of Gothic Thomism, Catholicism and Anglicanism," and "visualized social problems as mechanical relations similar to those of Newton's planetary universe. Laws were no longer based on spiritual realities but became human transactions freely entered into by the participants." God became as superfluous and as powerless as "the English monarch was in politics."[4]

I invariably find such arguments "conservative" in a very familiar and typical sense. That is, de Riencourt does not, in his invocation of spirituality, pull me back to Jesus or to the Gospels. He doesn't invoke the kingdom of God. Instead, he offers up the solid, substantial *social order* of the predemocratic West—a social hierarchy supposedly based comfortably and wisely on spiritual hierarchy—as the model by which to measure modern institutions and critique the modern temperament. It's not that this approach is totally devoid of ethical bite. Modern industrial democracy *is* morally shallow and brutally reductive. But democracy in its essence has been shaped by a variety of forces, the most elemental of which is a very human impulse to get out from under the oppressive authority of a person, or a system, that governs without the consent of the governed. The counterargument—that people are inherently unfit for self-governance—may be true, but it begs the question, the unspoken implication, that those who govern in a traditional hierarchy *are* miraculously fit not only for self-governance but for governance over others. Why that unspoken implication should be true for a self-selected few is either glossed over or explained in terms of sacred authority residing in the hierarchy itself, probably as deriving from God. It is a circular argument by which power justifies itself or points its finger skyward. It is not, in the end, a convincing or credible position.

So democracy rebels against smug, elite self-justification, and it rebels in the names of equality and fairness. But how ethically liberated, how fair and equal, *is* our democracy? When wealth inequality approximates the inequality operative in predemocratic societies, then we have to ask not only how we can claim to have anything resembling a functional democracy within a context of growing aristocratic wealth, but why we have come to this point, why democracy has not adequately addressed or resolved this problem of grossly unbalanced wealth concentration. Has democracy only liberated economic greed? A race to be rich? Is the lottery how we vote "democratically" (one ticket, one vote) for a chance to be instant aristocrats?

If democracy cannot go deeper into ethical self-governance, if it cannot grasp the fundamental need for servanthood and stewardship, then we would be better off, at least ecologically, with a restoration of explicit aristocracy and a corresponding reinstitution of a subsistent peasantry. Such a system would, quite possibly, be less ecologically toxic than capitalist globalization. But to subscribe to such a view, however, to insist that greater ethical depth is beyond us, or that the separation of church and state prevents even advocating for such depth because of original sin and because hierarchical governance is given by God to the secular state, is to fall into the so-called "conservative" camp, with sinful human nature unchangeable, and with otherworldly salvation our only hope for the realization of the kingdom of God. This has been, traditionally, the marriage of aristocratic prerogative with politically neutered religiosity, what Stringfellow calls the Constantinian Arrangement. Our supposedly democratic society has never shaken free of that marriage, and it is the church that has resisted any possible divorce. But we are reaching the end of that provisional and tentative liaison. Either we move beyond it, either our spirituality deepens into a politics of servanthood and stewardship, or we will see either global disaster or a restoration of explicit aristocratic rule. But such an aristocratic restoration would represent an absolutely monumental ethical failing, a political expression of spiritual contempt for the kingdom of God, a sin against the Holy Ghost—that is, a contemptuous refusal to acknowledge the spirituality of the Daughter, including the political tools of organization, structure, and theory as pointed out by Dorothee Soelle.

The kingdom of God, as articulated in the Gospels, has been (and continues to be) a huge problem for the overwhelmingly dominant theology of transcendence. If God is Out There in Elsewhere Land, then holy hierarchy logically follows and, with it, steep gradations in social class with corresponding deference to the class or classes above. Aristocracy is the logical outcome of an Elsewhere God. Otherworldly salvation is then the only hope worth clinging to. Earth is only to be endured. Democracy, with its dual promises of political equality and terrestrial groundedness, is, finally, a snare of the Devil—a mirage, an illusion, an evil fabrication.

That's not what I find at the heart of the Gospels. Instead, there's a passionate engagement with life, an amazingly earthy groundedness, all of it fully committed to servanthood and stewardship in the depths of a spirituality that recognizes Spirit *within* this moment, within this *person*, absolutely alive in *this* situation, on this *Earth*. Spirit is immanent, indwelling, bursting and bubbling with creative yearning, lovingly contemptuous of all exquisite rationalizations that purport to explain the divine supremacy of inherited doctrine and conditioned deference.

If Spirit—partly through the Gospels—really does work as salt, as yeast, as the least of seeds, then to deny and repudiate the transformation and growth of spiritual consciousness, heart, and equality is to deny Spirit, a sin against the Holy Spirit. The Constantinian Arrangement represents the righteous crystallizing of such sin—because it asserts that God provides and sustains empire—and the globalization of brutal civilization, with religious sanction, is its consequence. Not that Christianity invented or created civilization, but Christianity's doctrines of theological transcendence have heaped abuse and contempt on the insouciant immanence of Spirit, have fostered and justified aristocratic hubris, and have been, at best, condescendingly indifferent to the committed articulation of democratic and ecological governance boldly built on a foundation of servanthood and stewardship.[II]

II. For very readable expositions of the bitter conflict between "orthodox" and "gnostic" Christian camps prior to Constantine's authoritarian enforcement of a common creed, see Elaine Pagels' *The Gnostic Gospels* and *Beyond Belief*. If her analysis is substantially correct—that the "orthodox" were fiercely partisan in behalf of a common creed in order to consolidate ecclesiastical control, while the "gnostics" resisted such

The global crisis is fundamentally a crisis of perverse spirituality, of arrogant and oblivious human will rampant in Creation. Transcendence is a spiritual bulldozer heaping up disasters of Earth-sickening consequence. Righteous by theological tradition, by the prerogatives of elegant superiority, addicts of transcendence can only come to repentance by the suffering that lies patiently waiting in their blindness. Ecological oblivion is the shadow and consequence of otherworldly craving. Civilization has built the vehicle, but religion explains its godly purpose.

We have an enormous amount of civilizational and religious baggage to shed, to be disposed of in as ecological a manner as possible; and if we cannot achieve this shedding voluntarily, by means of repentance, we are destined to have that baggage crushed in the blowback of our disease-ridden traumatic institutions. So it's voluntary transformation or episodic (but accelerating and intensifying) catastrophes. That it's not an easy choice to make shows how deeply we are stuck in the ruts—in the orbits—of a distorted imperial spirituality that is both civilizational and religious.

---

consolidation in favor of ongoing, open-ended revelation—both camps seem to have missed (or "risen above") the multilayered dimensions of humility and wisdom contained within the kingdom of God proclamation. The "kingdom of God" does not figure largely in Pagels' two books, and this suggests "straight-thinking" doctrine versus esoteric mysticism had largely abandoned the powerfully grounded, astonishingly present Jesus in favor of contending brands of rationalization, one flat-footed and the other attempting to grow wings. To embrace the kingdom of God, even as it is a "concept" always beyond a person's capacity to understand, explain, or codify, remains the open doorway to the spirit of Jesus, to a temporal space paradoxically infused with an atmosphere of the eternal. But our capacity to live within the kingdom evaporates or disappears when our hearts or minds are hardened, when our beliefs (whether conventional or esoteric) steer our behavior and lock in our political structures in a two-kingdom manner. Jesus was amazingly open, although it was an openness saturated with love, brimming with compassion, and with an inerrant crap detector. In atomic terms, this is the nucleus we need to enter, perhaps through the eye of a needle. But, with our ego anxiety about risking such vulnerable openness, we are easily swung into spiritual orbit, giddily and frantically proclaiming orthodoxies or forms of esotery that either claim to have the real relics or know where they are symbolically hidden. Our collective religious consciousness lies largely in such orbits, and the institutionalization of those orbits makes it all normative, so that yearning for the nucleus is seen as an aberration and even as flirting with evil.

NOTES

1. Bacevich, "Semiwarriors," 33.
2. de Riencourt, *Coming*, 5.
3. Goodwyn, *Populist*, 319.
4. de Riencourt, *Coming*, 53.

12

One Last Little Thing

THERE'S A JOKE ABOUT musicians. How do you tell the difference between amateurs and professionals? You can't get professionals to start, and you can't get amateurs to stop. But this may be the last little thing. Perhaps. We'll see. Maybe we're all amateurs.

Norman O. Brown's *Life Against Death: The Psychoanalytical Meaning of History* is divided into six sections. The fifth section, "Studies in Anality," is subdivided into three chapters—"The Excremental Vision," "The Protestant Era," and "Filthy Lucre." It is from the second subset of "Filthy Lucre" ("Sacred and Secular") that I lift the following passage. In it Brown clarifies the labor theory of value:

> The value of money does not lie in the value with which the labor theory of value is concerned. And conversely—this is the crucial point—the labor theory of value does not contain the answer to the problem of power.
>
> The ultimate category of economics is power; but power is not an economic category. Marx fills up the emergent gap in his theory with the concept of force (violence)—i.e., by conceiving power as a material reality. We have argued elsewhere that this is a crucial mistake; power is in essence a psychological category. And to pursue the tracks of power, we will have to enter the domain of the sacred, and map it: all power is essentially sacred power.[1]

Power is psychological. Power is sacred. I think we have here (I especially recommend "The Protestant Era" and "Filthy Lucre") an essential insight that goes a long way toward explaining the willful, stubborn captivity of mainstream Christianity to civilization, a captivity to power, a "Constantinian Arrangement," a subtle but profound shift from kingdom of God consciousness to empire acquiescence that is the direct ancestor of the Christian Right today—but not only the Christian Right.

Kingdom of God consciousness is "not of this world" primarily in the sense that it stands in opposition to predatory civilizational power. It is not of the predatory "worldly" power represented by the false spirituality of civilized governance. Kingdom of God consciousness is truly at home in Creation, fully granting the ambiguities and uncertainties inherent in mortality and death, as well as the essential mystery of our incarnational consciousness.[1] "Not of this world" was quickly bent into Earth-denying, otherworldly craving, into heavenly lust, and that impulse, as far as I can understand, is based on the fear of ego dissolution and/or eternal punishment. That is, the desperate glomming onto heaven with a compulsive grip has as its psychological basis a desperate fear, a fear of personal extinction or perpetual agony.

But we are all going to die. We may talk about death as the "enemy" all we want, but if death is an enemy then so is birth. And if in heaven there is neither birth nor death, then there are no flowers in heaven—at least not the sort of flowers I know—because flowers need dirt, and dirt is made of excrement and death. Life on Earth in all its fantastic variety rests on an immense ecological bank account of soil, of death and decay. It is this enormous reservoir of amassed nutrients and energy on which we depend for every breath and heartbeat. In the end, our body wastes—and our very bodies—return to this reserve, even if we humans have invented ways—from flush toilets to concrete casket boxes—to temporarily thwart or distort the restorative process. But nature is patient, and always wins. Or, to push the point more personally, whatever comes after my death is totally out of my control. If something of me—of my consciousness or body—lives on, or persists, or is resurrected, then so be it. If not, not. In a very real and important way, that's not my concern. That's God's job, not mine. If I am to believe in God, that belief simply has to be built on a scaf-

---

I. In a footnote on page 289, Spengler in his *Decline* asserts that it is the eschatological treatise of Mark 13 that reveals the "apocalyptic character of Jesus' daily discourses." On the previous page, Spengler insists that "To ascribe social purposes to Jesus is a blasphemy." This is amusing on several levels. First, Spengler's "organic succession" is completely naturalistic. Such a construction has or needs no God, although "Prime Mover" may serve as a useful social convention or ideological mascot. Therefore Spengler's use of the word "blasphemy"—something profane or mocking of God—is mere bogieman semantics. Spengler's assertions imply that Jesus was essentially contemptuous of Creation, had no hope for a spiritual transformation of human consciousness and human behavior on Earth, and could hardly wait for otherworldly vindication. And that, I'm afraid, is both funny and pathetic.

fold less rickety than my personal fear of hanging. That is, the "God" who supposedly rescues me from nature, from the foundational recycling process of Creation, seems suspiciously to be a first-responder fantasy arising from anxiety in the face of what is certainly the eventual extinction of provisional consciousness and identity. Am I really supposed to balance my entire spirituality on the point of this religious thumbtack?

If not, what is my task? Well, a good part so far has been attempting to peel off the ecclesiastical bandages that were stuck on me by centuries of righteous Christian doctrine—all those magnificent men in their gorgeous robes and ardent articulations who *really knew* the inside skinny of God's Plan and Creation's Mystery. Trying to locate an actual Jesus behind and through all that religious gauze—or Spenglerian fog—has been a long process and (who knows whether or to what extent I've succeeded?) what I've found there is an extraordinarily alive and brave man who said "The system sucks. You who rule are a bunch of crooks, frauds, cowardly bullies, and sanctimonious quacks. If you really want to get with God's Program, here's what you need to do: renounce your predatory power, abandon advantage, eschew violence, love God with all your heart (not just with your pandering political speech) and love your neighbor (including that alleged Islamofascist living down the street) as you love yourself." By lusting after an otherworldly heaven, Christians felt compelled to suck up to an awesome transcendent God in the hope of obtaining a winning Elsewhere ticket. Part of understanding such a God was to fear His unsurpassing power. And, in a hierarchical society, the emperor obviously derived *his* power directly from this God. Therefore fearing God and obeying emperor were linked mandates, complementary obligations. Skepticism regarding one suggested skepticism of the other. Disobedience of one implied disobedience of the other.

Early Christians took their eye off the ball. They let go the humble, difficult kingdom of God, went chasing after otherworldly salvation, and fell into the cynical arms of a smirking Caesar posturing as the Heavenly Father's right-hand man. So here we are, seventeen centuries later, with so-called Christian Zionists helping to plot the end of the world so heavenly salvation can come as a ball of fire, stoking world-destroying catastrophe so the Prince of Peace can return with a sword in his mouth!

All power is essentially sacred power said Norman O. Brown, a very brilliant psychoanalytical theologian. So, if you are searching for God, the place to look is within the Creation-based ethical practicalities of Jesus.

That's where you'll find the kingdom of God, and that may be all the salvation we'll ever need. Or, if it's not all we'll ever need, it's what we need to master first, before we're spiritually qualified to proceed to other—perhaps otherworldly—orbits.

NOTES

1. Brown, *Life*, 251.

13

At the Foot of the Lord's Castle

O<small>N</small> M<small>ONDAY</small>, M<small>AY</small> 21, 2007, I gave to my friend David Kast what I believed to be the remainder of these provocations (he had the first five or so), and I gave to David's daughter Nicole a provisionally complete manuscript to read, to take with her to Mexico, to share with Gustavo Esteva at the Universidad de la Tierra en Oaxaca. Nikki, in turn, gave me a copy of a small book by Gustavo, entitled *Celebration of Zapatismo,* his reflections on the meaning of the Zapatista rebellion in Chiapas. This morning (May 27—the calendar either appropriately or mockingly tells me it's the liturgical day of Pentecost), having finished Gustavo's *Celebration,* with no apparent flame hovering above my head, I will begin an addendum—done in time, I hope, for Nikki to take with her to Oaxaca, when she leaves in early June.

Here is the question around which *Celebration of Zapatismo* revolves: "Can there be such a thing as a revolutionary group with no interest in seizing power?"[1] That, says Gustavo, is the question at the heart of the Zapatista movement. Later, Gustavo quotes the following passage from an essay by Wolfgang Sachs:

> Ever since the apostle Paul had shattered the validity of worldly distinctions in the face of God's gift of salvation, it had become thinkable to conceive of all humans as standing on the same plane. The Enlightenment secularized this heritage and turned it into a humanist creed. Neither class nor sex, neither religion nor race count before human nature, as they didn't count before God. Thus the universality of the Sonship of God was recast as the universality of human dignity. From then on, "humanity" became the common denominator uniting all peoples, causing differences in skin color, beliefs and social customs to decline in significance.[2]

And then Gustavo immediately says this: "Accepting the assumption that there is a fundamental sameness in all human beings, the construction of *One World* was adopted in the West as a moral obligation."[3]

This formulation regarding "fundamental sameness" makes me uneasy. It's not that fundamental sameness isn't a consequence of aggressive One World ideology—just think of blue jeans or Coca-Cola—it's that the driving force for One World has not been a horizontal celebration of sameness but, totally contrary, the vertical imposition of unlikeness, of superiority. Gustavo must be confusing the material outcome of industrial mass production with the aggressive force of aristocratic civility hiding within nominally "democratic" institutions. And contrary to Wolfgang Sachs' assertion that the Enlightenment secularized the heritage of all humans standing on the same plane, historian George Mosse, in his *Toward the Final Solution*, says that "Eighteenth-century Europe was the cradle of modern racism," a cradle built not only on Euro-Christian racist views but also on "aesthetic criteria derived from ancient Greece," with the subsequent "pseudo-sciences of physiognomy and phrenology."[4] These "pseudo-sciences" did not produce a "same plane" but, rather, brutal depictions of racial difference and ethnic inferiority. The "universal culturicide"[5] Gustavo laments, hidden under the cloak of globalization, derives in large part from the spiritual, ethical, and moral *superiority* of Christian doctrine, with its explicit otherworldly disregard for life on Earth, and that doctrine's subsequent fusion with Roman Empire imperialism— and, then, the politics of the West deriving from that fusion, complete with reverence for the Greek ideal. Christian civilization has sought the conversion—and conquest—of the world not just because everybody is the same, but precisely because so many others are (or were) *unlike* and *inferior*. The Christian program was a mission of spiritual uplift and civilizational elevation. "Fundamental sameness" also requires a political program. In the present world, sameness has been immensely increased by technological commercialism inclusive of the fabricating process, the management process, and the educational process. But "sameness" derives from the imposition of uniform (or orthodox) superiority. To read, for instance, Elaine Pagels' books *The Gnostic Gospels* and *Beyond Belief* is to see how the absolutely fierce drive of so many of the pre-Constantinian "church fathers" to achieve enforceable doctrinal orthodoxy was based thoroughly on a complete conviction of superior understanding.

Orthodox means to have the correct opinion; in a system of totalitarian enforcement, orthodoxy requires sameness.[1]

So when the author of Romans 13 says in verse 1, "Let every person render obedience to the governing authorities; for there is no authority except from God, and those in authority are divinely constituted, so that the rebel against the authority is resisting God's appointment," this is an obvious prelude to Augustine's assertion that kingdoms and empires are given by God. Yet all this is in total contradiction to the account in the Old Testament (1 Samuel 8) where the prophet Samuel condemns the elders of Israel, and spells out the dreadful consequences, when the elders come to him wanting a king; and, even more, when Jesus refuses all the kingdoms of the world from the *hand of the Devil* in the temptation scenes (Matthew 4 and Luke 4), and then goes on to announce the arrival of the kingdom of God in which the last are to be first, where only servants can be leaders, where nonviolence, voluntary poverty, and love of enemies are the ethical thresholds to be crossed in order to enter and actually live within the kingdom of God.

The "sameness" that aggravates Gustavo does not begin as "democratic" doctrine. It begins as civilized contempt for the noncivilized, as religious hypertension, and it is further empowered by a civilized/reli-

---

I. Theologian John B. Cobb, Jr., in "Spiritual Paradigms of the Western World and Non-Western Alternatives," pages 50 through 66, walks us through the changes in Western Europe from the legacy of Greece to the Roman Empire to what he calls "Christianism" to nationalism to economism. Since Cobb believes Earth "cannot survive three hundred years of economism, much less a thousand," he advocates, with some hesitation, what he calls "Earthism"—a "primal vision" and "deep commitment" to the Earth, a "new religion" and a "new spirituality" that no longer accepts economism as an adequate philosophy of life.

In Christian terms, Cobb (apparently following Tillich) identifies "Christianism" as the claim by the church to "represent" God and "speak for God." Cobb sees this claim as a fundamental distortion of devotion. But he makes no mention of the kingdom of God, and he nowhere even hints at the bubbling yeastiness of Spirit. Although he opens his essay with comments on the understanding of history with which he was raised and nurtured—that *real* history only began with cities and civilization, that uncivilized people were "savages" and "hardly human," that "true" history was the history of Western Europe and North America, that women were not participants in this history, and that these intellectual and spiritual energies continue to represent "the forces that control the world today"—he implies but never frankly says it's male-warrior civilization that's killing us. Why isn't he more explicit and forthcoming? The answer must remain speculative, but I presume it has to do with Cobb's doubt that the kingdom of God or Gospel or Spirit is sufficiently strong to dissolve or transform the utopian angularities of civilization into the eutopian roundedness of resurrected folk evolution.

gious imperialism that, by the fourth century, articulates its contempt in the epithet of "paganism," a curse formalizing in a religious sense not only the cultural inferiority of rural people but their inherent spiritual wickedness—"hardly human," in the words of John Cobb. Such sameness as is eventually produced in the Western world is the standardized, perverse sameness of triumphant civilized superiority, an empty, standardized sameness that is the uniform "cultural" residue remaining when multiform folk behavior is extinguished, manifested in our time through the industrialized commodities of capitalist "development" and the service institutions (especially schools) that Ivan Illich so vigorously attacked. Wolfgang Sachs, in the same essay from which Gustavo extracts a passage, also says this:

> Just as Christians had their heathens, philosophers of the Enlightenment had their savages. Both figures embodied the negation of what the respective societies held as their self-images. Heathens were those outside the Kingdom of God, while savages lived outside the kingdom of civilization. But there was one crucial difference. Whereas for Christendom heathens populated geographically remote areas, for the Enlightenment savages inhabited an infant stage of history. Europe of the Enlightenment no longer felt separated from the Other spatially, but chronologically. As a matter of fact, the existence of strange peoples like the Iroquois, Asante or Bengali at the borders of (European) civilization contradicted the very idea of one mankind. But the contradiction was resolved by interpreting the multiplicity of cultures in space as a succession of stages in time. So the 'savage' was defined as one who would grow up and enter the stage of civilization. The 'savage,' though he lived now, was assigned the status of a child in the biography of mankind, a child which was not yet fully mature, and was in need of guidance by a strong father.[6]

Although there is real insight here, I quibble—if quibble it is—over Sachs' use of the term "Kingdom of God." I don't think the church said heathens were outside the kingdom of God. The civilized church has tended to simply ignore the kingdom of God. The church said heathens were *doomed to Hell* unless, through conversion, they accepted salvation as offered by and through the church, unless they professed belief in its doctrines and teachings. The "need of guidance by a strong father" was not only aimed at the savage caught in an early stage of development—i.e., the not yet civilized—but also at the heathen who had to be persuaded (or coerced) to bow before the emperor and the all-powerful Christian Father. This combination of civilized and religious Father adoration is what lies behind the "strict father" model of politics that the Berkeley linguist George Lakoff has popularized, a model that obviously has continued to undergird the fusion of corporate power and Christian "moral values," the kind of politics that characterizes the so-called neoconservative Right.

I've also gone back to Norman O. Brown's cryptic and aphoristic *Love's Body*. Here, on the opening page of the first chapter (called "Liberty"), we find that:

> Freud's myth of the rebellion of the sons against the father in the primal, prehistoric horde is not a historical explanation of origins, but a supra-historical archetype; eternally recurrent; a myth; an old, old story.
>
> Freud seems to project into prehistoric times the constitutional crisis of seventeenth-century England. The primal father is *absolute monarch* of the horde; the females are his *property*. The sons form a *conspiracy* to *overthrow* the despot, and in the end substitute a *social contract* with *equal rights* for all. This anachronistic history directs us to look for the recurrence of the archetype in the seventeenth century.[7]

But this is less a problem of projecting seventeenth-century England back into prehistoric times than a problem of projecting the entire archetype of civilization (or civilizational rule) into prehistoric times. Brown goes on to say that the foundation of the state is *the* primal crime, a fraternal crime, an act of juvenile delinquency, and the social contract is the "form of sworn covenant," a "socializing sacrilege," an oath both curse and sacred sacrilege.[8] We may well continue to argue about "original sin," about what the construct does or doesn't mean, but it's certainly time we began to have a serious discussion about the foundation of the state, of civilization, resting on primal crime and fraternal oath.

So when Ivan Illich, in the last essay ("The Cultivation of Conspiracy") in *The Challenges of Ivan Illich,* says that "The European idea of peace that is synonymous with the somatic incorporation of equals into a community of equals has no analogue elsewhere," and then goes on to say "Community in our European tradition is not the outcome of an act of authoritative foundation, nor a gift from nature or its gods, nor the result of management, planning, and design, but the consequence of a *conspiracy*, a deliberate, mutual, somatic, and gratuitous gift to one another," how are we to understand his assertions? "No analogue elsewhere" does seem to smack of spiritual privilege, of something totally unique, and of religious superiority. This *conspiracy*, Illich continues, has its prototype in the "celebration of the early Christian liturgy."[9] By using an elusive middle term like "liturgy," Illich may mean either a Zapatista-like desire for an earthly kingdom of God or an Augustinian desire for heavenly immortal disembodiment. Illich goes on to say that the idea of a social contract, since at least the fourteenth century, has its concrete origins in the *conspiratio*:

> The medieval merchants and craftsmen who settled at the foot of a lord's castle felt the need to make the conspiracy that united them into a secure and lasting association. To provide for their general surety, they had recourse to a device, the *conjuratio*, a mutual promise confirmed by an oath that uses God as a witness. Most societies know the oath, but the use of God's name to make it stick first appears as a legal device in the codification of Roman law made by the Christian emperor Theodosius. Conjuration, or the swearing together by a common oath confirmed by the invocation of God, just like the liturgical *osculum*, is of Christian origin. The *conjuratio* that uses God as epoxy for the social bond presumably assures stability and durability to the atmosphere engendered by the *conspiratio* of the citizens. In this linkage between *conspiratio* and *conjuratio*, two equally unique concepts inherited from the first millennium of Christian history are intertwined, but the contractual formality soon overshadowed the spiritual substance.
>
> The medieval town of central Europe was indeed a profoundly new historical gestalt; the *conjuratio conspirativa* makes European urbanity distinct from urban modes elsewhere. It also implies a peculiar dynamic strain between the atmosphere of *conspiratio* and its legal, contractual constitution. Ideally, the spiritual climate is the source of the city's life that flowers into a hierarchy, like a shell or frame, to protect its order. Insofar as the city is understood to originate in *conspiratio*, it owes its social existence to the *pax*, the breath, shared equally among all.[10]

But, as Norman O. Brown says, "Every oath is sacred sacrilege, like the primal crime itself."[11] Illich may obscurely imply this when he talks about God as glue, epoxy for the social bond. But who is this gluey God? Is this God the Epoxy King who can fix anything or everything? The God who can give kingdoms and empires? If so, as Brown says, "The patriarchal family supplies the primal model for political government: the first form of government is kingship, 'because families are always monarchically governed'; the essence of government is domination, 'rule'—in the family the domination of male over female, parent over child, master over slave."[12] Do we therefore conjure up a conspiratorial contract in order to engender a hierarchy to protect the city's order? Is this anything more than endless cycle, an eternal recurrence of sons versus fathers and fathers versus sons? (And there is, of course, a fierce objection to oaths of all kinds, beyond a simple yes or no, in Matthew 5:33–37.) Is the Daughter coming to end this game of male oath-taking?

So, to my friend Gustavo (whom I've not yet met in person) I say this: If there is no bubbling Spirit carbonating within, the Zapatistas are only a new turning of an old, old wheel. But if there *is* Spirit (whether or not it was smuggled out of Israel by Christian proselytizers and refugees, whether or not—"no analogue elsewhere"—it sneaked into medieval European cities prior to stowing away on ships teeming with conquistadors), then maybe the Zapatistas have a chance at stimulating revolution with no interest in seizing power. If so, this bubbly Spirit is no epoxy God. She can't be conjured up by sacred sacrilege or bouts of male bonding at tailgate parties at God's Super Bowl. Yeast, maybe, or virus. The smallest and least of seeds. A stowaway in the heart.

But this implies something else. We have to be willing and able to be in the presence, the atmosphere, the radiant embrace of this Spirit; we have to trust Her wholesomeness; we have to submit to Her purifications; we have to accept Her spiritual humility; we have to voluntarily imitate Her leastness. Just because there's no viable option to this trust, submission, acceptance, and embrace doesn't mean we will choose this path, however. The only thing we know for sure is that this *is* the path to choose.

NOTES

1. Esteva, *Celebration*, 9.
2. Esteva, *Celebration*, 33.
3. Esteva, *Celebration*, 33.
4. Mosse, *Toward*, 1, 2, 5.
5. Esteva, *Celebration*, 33.
6. Sachs, *Development*, 104.
7. Brown, *Love's*, 3.
8. Brown, *Love's*, 16.
9. Illich, "Cultivation," 241.
10. Illich, "Cultivation," 241.
11. Brown, *Love's*, 17.
12. Brown, *Love's*, 8.

14

This New Place

M Y FRIEND DAVID KAST has given me a number of books over the years, including a copy of the late Edward Said's *Culture and Imperialism*. An inside page, in the front, tells the reader that Said was an internationally renowned literary and cultural critic, a professor at Columbia University, and the author of more than twenty books. I had known of Said through his occasional writings in *The Nation*. Those writings tended to be dense and complex, not exactly what one thinks of as journalism. So it is with *Culture and Imperialism*. Said's topic here is the relationship between literary culture and imperial aggression in Western Europe and America, roughly from the nineteenth to the late twentieth century (though many references slide farther back in time), and his thesis is that literary culture and imperialism are nowhere as separate or as disconnected as convention has made them out to be.

Said enters this fray as a brilliant outsider—by birth and upbringing a Palestinian Christian, an Arab, a person who embraced much of Western culture (he apparently was an excellent pianist who especially loved Beethoven), but also a person who, by virtue of his ethnicity, found it easy to identify with other intellectuals from diverse continents and countries who were striving to find (and assert) authentic personhood as—what shall we call them?—aggrieved children of colonialism and its anticolonial aftermath. It is this outsider sensitivity that Said brings into his analysis. Here I want to quote a passage from *Culture and Imperialism* and then suggest, if I can, a critical parallel:

> We live of course in a world not only of commodities but also of representation, and representations—their production, circulation, history, and interpretation—are the very element of culture. In much recent theory the problem of representation is deemed to be central, yet rarely is it put in its full political context, a context

that is primarily imperial. Instead we have on the one hand an isolated cultural sphere, believed to be freely and unconditionally available to weightless theoretical speculation and investigation, and, on the other, a debased political sphere, where the real struggle between interests is supposed to occur. To the professional student of culture—the humanist, the critic, the scholar—only one sphere is relevant, and, more to the point, it is accepted that the two spheres are separated, whereas the two are not only connected but ultimately the same.

A radical falsification has become established in this separation. Culture is exonerated of any entanglements with power, representations are considered only as apolitical images to be parsed and construed as so many grammars of exchange, and the divorce of the present from the past is assumed to be complete. And yet, far from this separation of spheres being a neutral or accidental choice, its real meaning is as an act of complicity, the humanist's choice of a disguised, denuded, systematically purged textual model over a more embattled model, whose principal features would inevitably coalesce around the continuing struggle over the question of empire itself.[1]

It strikes me that what Edward Said is identifying as a "radical falsification" in cultural analysis—that tender culture is supposedly exonerated of any sordid entanglements with raw and brutal power—is a secularized version of the Christian doctrine of the two kingdoms: that God mandated separate entities of church and state, that the church (like literary culture) is God's clean hand and the state (like imperial power or aggression) is God's dirty hand, and that each is free of entanglement with the other. The two assertions—the cultural one and the religious one—certainly are parallel. We might even say that Said's image is an inversion of Pontius Pilate's famous gesture. That is, instead of benign empire washing its hands of complicity with religious cruelty, as we see with Pilate in John 19, what we see instead, through Said's keen discernment, is culture piously washing *its* hands of any sordid affiliation with the cruelties of imperialism.

What's easy to see, then, if one has eyes to see, is how the radical falsification of this separation in both culture and religion has enabled a perpetual and normative schizophrenia in the underlying structure of acquiescence. I mean by this the acquiescence that pervades everyday life. I mean in particular the ethical vacuity of the churches. I mean especially how churches, in principle the only truly independent set of "public" institutions established precisely on the moral, ethical, and spiritual articulation of unconditional truth, are instead, in bulk, that institutional force most likely to mobilize consent for imperial adventures, urge (or at least be complicit with) the suppression of dissent, and fan the flames of a blind, unhesitating patriotism: standing fast for the validity and integrity of God's other hand. This falsification is certainly galling in the area of cultural studies (Edward Said elegantly writes out his insightful exasperations), but hypocrisy has more room to hide, more costumes to wear, in the imperial closet of *Realpolitik*. Ethical clarity comes there on a sliding scale governed by political "necessity." We hardly expect political "truth" to be anything besides bizarre and bent images in a hall of distorted mirrors, manipulated "reflections" designed to secure popular consent or acquiescence as politicians pander to corporate power or to some grand fantasy of their historic stature.

Falsification is more deeply poisonous when it comes to religion, however, and especially in regard to the Christian doctrine of two kingdoms. Christianity claims, at least in its more "conservative" forms, to be *the* lucid and honest way of being in the world, with a depth of altered and cleansed consciousness attained through recognition of its sins, its heartfelt repentance, and its repeated divine forgiveness—a consciousness that has passed repeatedly through the eye of a spiritual needle, with that needle centered in the ethical purity of the person Jesus, the Jesus who proclaimed the kingdom of God, the Jesus of nonviolence, voluntary poverty, and radical servanthood, the fellow who washed other people's feet and asked us to love our enemies. Christians who subscribe to the doctrine of two kingdoms have found a way to evade (or at least to minimize) the radical nonviolent servanthood of this Jesus. This evasion is most keenly made manifest by the allocating of violence to the state, a much-hallowed theological maneuver by which the pious Christian (more or less like Pontius Pilate) can wash his religious hand of deadly violence because God has mandated the exercise of violence to his other hand. Among believing Christians, this betrayal of the kingdom of God is often in inverse proportion to their fervent affirmation of Christ as Lord and Savior. That is, the demands of the everyday ethical are systematically eschewed, especially at the level of public policy—questions of war, military spending, ecocidal weaponry, poverty and wealth, economic exploitation, rates of incarceration, racism, "terrorist" detention centers, the vast inequalities in healthcare, excessive industrialization, deepening ecological fractures, rural culture exhaustion, climate change, etc., etc.—in favor of (in cultural terms) lifestyle maintenance and (in religious terms) a kind of supernatural steroid confidence in afterlife salvation. The real meaning of culture and religion claiming exoneration from any sordid entanglements with power ramifies as an act of complicity, a pleasant, contented, largely conflict-free array of shallow convictions and daily habits that keep at bay any troubled considerations of empire, of how we are its beneficiaries, of what it might mean to love the enemy, to be a servant or the least, or how we might begin to undo the prevailing structures of domination under the stealthy wings of a permanent war economy and begin to actually wrestle with the grounded practicalities of what we might call an ecological economy.

There is, without question, a tendency toward evasion in every one of us. We might even call it the normal human condition. Not only is there a tendency toward evasion, we all carry our baggage of evasion with us through life. While some of us simply refuse to acknowledge any evasiveness, either because of doctrinal or psychological reasons, or because of some designer blend peculiar to each of us as individuals, others of us (guilty liberals?) more or less recognize our evasions but feel powerless to undo them. We feel structurally locked in, we are lazy, afraid, we lack examples of how to break out, we rationalize our evasion as the lesser evil, especially at election time. We might yet do differently, but right now we're too young and inexperienced. We might have done differently, but now we're too old and set in our ways.[I]

Something pretty monstrous happens, I think, when evasion swamps ethically sturdy perspectives—as we saw, for example, in the Joe McCarthy period in the early 1950s, or in the (obviously still lingering) aftermath of 9/11. As I have tried to articulate in these little essays, the magnitude and consequence of evasion deepens and thickens as the base is taken up into the superstructure, as exploited people, oppositional groups, or previously excluded classes are drawn into civilizational mythology and empire complicity.[II] Nationalism is therefore hugely strengthened not

I. For a very thoughtful and provocative exploration of this issue in an explicitly ethical context (whose epigraph might be "maximum individuality *within* maximum community"), see Part III, "The Ideal-Type: The Individual and the Community," pages 249 through 303, in Ernest Becker's *The Structure of Evil.*

II. The ability to put oneself in another person's consciousness is, obviously, difficult if not downright slippery. And while we may not be able to do this with any great certainty in a strictly personal sense, we are foolish and perhaps even stupid if we believe that *our* consciousness, *my* consciousness, is absolutely normative. When George Mosse, only by the lethality of weapons and their abundance due to economic affluence and technological innovation, but also by the inclusion of huge numbers of marginalized people, people who now begin to reflexively identify with the flag rather than ignore or scorn it. This process accelerates as thoughtful dialogue is flooded by barking propaganda and flashing electronic media. Plus we are living in a time when the civilizational superstructure is, as the United States likes to assert, not only the only option that's materially viable but the only option that's morally worthy of spiritual allegiance. In this circumstance, one hardly looks for or expects real opposition or tough spiritual diagnoses from the church, except for Catholic Workers, a certain slice of the traditional "peace churches" (Brethren, Mennonite, and Quaker), and a tiny "radicalized" minority within mainstream denominations. I think the point here is that evasion became ideologically rationalized in the church as early as Romans 13. It certainly was institutionally locked into place with the Constantinian Arrangement. Otherworldly salvation became the overriding preoccupation of the church, and the kingdom of God, as the viral, yeasty, creeping spiritual infection of servanthood and stewardship, was condemned as false or misplaced devotion—or simply ignored and left to wither on the vine. This condemnation implicates all Left-leaning economic proposals ("Better dead than Red") as structural sharing was eventually associated

---

for instance, says on page 6 of his *Final Solution* that, toward the end of the eighteenth century, there were "pragmatic [social] changes which seemed to set men adrift," we need to go on to a scholar like E. J. Hobsbawm to get a deeper understanding of what those changes were and how they affected human consciousness, especially in the lower classes. For this we have an amazingly insightful chapter ("The Human Results of the Industrial Revolution 1750–1850") in Hobsbawm's *Industry and Empire.* In it (pages 79 through 95) Hobsbawm says the Industrial Revolution represents a *"fundamental social change"* (his italics), something that "destroyed . . . old ways of living"—although Hobsbawm states clearly that the British gentry, the Church of England, and the universities fared quite well. It was, he says, the "labouring poor . . . whose traditional world and way of life the Industrial Revolution destroyed, without automatically substituting anything else. It is this disruption which is at the heart of the question about the social effects of industrialization." Hobsbawm goes on to list four ways in which industrial labor differs from preindustrial life: no income except a cash wage; "a regularity, routine and monotony quite unlike pre-industrial rhythms of work" (the "tyranny of the clock"); the shift from countryside to city; and the "conflict between the 'moral economy' of the past and the economic rationality of the capitalist present." All this, says Hobsbawm, "reflected not merely material poverty but social pauperization: the destruction of old ways of life without the substitution of anything the labouring poor could regard as a satisfactory equivalent."

with atheistic secular power, with evil and the Devil, much as ecological alarm gets repudiated as heathenistic "earthism." With the enemy identified as the pagan (along with socialists, tree huggers, homosexuals, and feminists), it's easy to see how the church's historic fulminations against "paganism"—that is, against that class (the peasantry) from which Jesus arose and whose "moral economy" was, for all practical purposes, closest in actual practice to the ethical prescriptions of servanthood and stewardship—provided much of the intellectual groundwork by which First World imperialism eventually rationalized and justified its economic exploitation and cultural wreckage of the Third World. ("We had to destroy the village in order to save it.") Western civilization has long been married to righteous Christianity. Cultural imperialism and religious imperialism share a well-fused worldview, a worldview seriously and willfully blind to its structural evasions and to the blithe hubris of its presumption—that is, its "innocent" consciousness. "Development" as global mission has therefore had both civilized and religious underpinnings.

The church is deeply compromised with civilizational suppositions, its complicity with evasion so old, venerable, and doctrinally institutionalized that one would be shocked to hear Gospel preached with fervor from the pulpit or the kingdom of God proclaimed with sincere conviction. Apply Edward Said's cultural critique to the church, pack the two together, observe their interlocking radical falsification as this falsification ramifies historically, attend to its sheer power, its weaponry, its zealous fanaticism, its ecologically deranging technologies, its demonization of critical appraisals—and one would be foolish to imagine a Happy Ending, despite what Edward Said, in cultural terms, calls "an internationalist counter-articulation."[2]

We are, I believe, approaching End Times, though I don't believe this is the end times conventionally understood. (The conventionally understood End Times draws its apocalyptic picture from its bulging sack of structural evasions, from biblical literalism, and from coloring book mythology.) If civilization congealed roughly five thousand years ago, and if its radical falsification is inherent in its schizophrenic predatory structure ("diseases" and "traumatic institutions"), and if its institutional corruption lies behind what William Stringfellow called the Constantinian Arrangement (an arrangement that institutionalized the pre-existing evasive tendencies within Christianity and deflected its critical gaze from empire to "the pagan," from kingdom of God transformation to otherworldly salvation), and if civilization in its Western industrialized mode has essentially wrecked all indigenous and peasant cultures worldwide, then we have reached an absolutely new place in human evolution on Earth. This new place as currently configured is simply not sustainable. Something has to give. Therefore it's either unmitigated global catastrophe, restoration of explicit aristocracy, or the founding of a radically new Something. The requisite elements are there for the advent of each of these three. Weapons (not to mention climate changes) are in place for catastrophe; aristocratic presumption is in the economic and political ascendant; and twenty million people around the world were on the streets to protest the U.S. invasion of Iraq in 2003, many of them (I think) fully willing to make do without civilization and return (if "return" is what we call it) to noncivilized folk culture evolution, with a painfully realized commitment to economic sharing and ecological reverence, a restoration, perhaps, of an organic process suppressed and thwarted by armed male warrior energy at the core of "civilized values," at the center of civilization itself. When Edward Said says "The executive presence is central in American culture today: the president, the television commentator, the corporate official, celebrity. Centrality is identity, what is powerful, important, and *ours*," he is implicitly affirming the civilizational analysis, for civilization is "executive presence" supreme.[3] "Globalization" is its hegemony over all the Earth.[III]

The kingdom of God is spiritually incompatible with the falsification exemplified by civilization and civilized religion. (The doctrine of two kingdoms may be *the* linchpin that locks civilization to civilized religion, for it forcibly guarantees the spurning of the kingdom of God as ongoing social unfolding as it accords free governance—perpetual "executive presence"—to the state.) But I think the kingdom of God has, despite dismissive rejection and contemptuous abandonment by the ecclesia, a

---

III. For a very hard-nosed appraisal of Barack Obama's first year as president, see Roger Hodge's "The Mendacity of Hope" in the February 2010 issue of *Harper's*, pages 7 through 11, even though Hodge's larger theme is "America's liberal empire and executive monarchism" that were "nurtured together in the womb of the Republic." In other words, Hodge sees Obama as just another imperial president methodically expanding and defending American globalization, all of it fully padded with the usual lofty rhetoric. Hodge also, to some extent, answers Jonathan Schell's question about the source of "this right-wing veto" that was pondered in a footnote in the ninth essay; this "veto" is rooted in empire lust and is neither right-wing nor left-wing in the conventional use of the terms, but engulfs both.

running shot at transforming whatever may be the flaws, failures, and foibles of folk evolution. The kingdom of God may be the only kind of spiritual energy capable of lifting folk evolution from its encrusted civilized impoundment while also liberating it from its gender and tribal limitations.

Plus there's always that mischievous lurking Spirit who will, I believe, really surprise us. The "kingdom" will be embodied by a democratic "Queen" or a "Princess"—or, far more in keeping with the overall ethos of the democratic kingdom of God, a melding of Martha the housekeeper and Mary the intellectual (Luke 10:38–42), with the tough and independent Samaritan woman at the well (John 4:5–21), and with the erotic wholesomeness of the unnamed woman in Luke 7:36–50 who loves Jesus with an unashamed sensuality. We men, meanwhile, will have to find something more creative to do with our restless egos and bubbling testosterone than load spaceships for God or prepare missiles for launch against Allah. Astonishingly, we might actually learn to really *live* on Earth simultaneously with the discovery of a far deeper and richer erotic tenderness. Imagine that.

NOTES

1. Said, *Culture*, 56–57.
2. Said, *Culture*, 311.
3. Said, *Culture*, 324.

15

The End of This Road

JOHN B. JUDIS, WRITING in the August 27, 2007, issue of *The New Republic*, weaves two strands of thought in his "Death Grip." First, he reports his puzzlement over white blue-collar workers (in this instance from Martinsburg, West Virginia) who voted against their own economic interests by casting their ballots for George W. Bush, and then he slides into an exploration of the work of three psychologists (Sheldon Solomon, Jeff Greenberg, and Tom Pyszcynski) who have developed a theory, supported by lots of experiments, that "goes a long way toward unraveling the mystery" of white working-class voting patterns.[1] The core of this new theory, according to Judis, is that "the mere thought of one's mortality can trigger a range of emotions—from disdain for other races, religions, and nations, to a preference for charismatic over pragmatic leaders, to heightened attraction to traditional mores."[1]

I've just read Marcus Borg's *The Heart of Christianity*, which is largely an analysis of the two major trends within contemporary Christianity. We might call those trends conservative versus liberal or literalist versus metaphorical. The most stimulating chapter in Borg's book is "The Kingdom of God: The Heart of Justice." In it, Borg revisits his prior analysis of Christianity as otherworldly salvationism versus Christianity as personal, communal, social, and political transformation. One of the biblical scholars Borg periodically quotes is John Dominic Crossan. But here (footnote 9 from the "Kingdom of God" chapter) Borg quotes from

---

I. Always provocative and insightful (if also limited by what seems an upper middle-class removal from folk reality), Kevin Phillips in *Bad Money: Reckless Finance, Failed Politics, and the Global Crisis of American Capitalism* is an equal opportunity critic of both Republicans and Democrats. On page 157, he says both parties have "uprooted themselves from what were their constituencies and allegiances as late as the 1960s," and he excoriates both parties for their weddedness to financial and business elites. "For both parties, the bottom line is usually the same: *the bottom line*. Fund raising. Money."

Crossan's *Excavating Jesus*: "Be it called the Kingdom of God or Heaven, it means the divine will for this earth, for here below, for here and now. How, in other words, would God run the world if God sat on Caesar's throne?"[2]

I've recently read Crossan's new book *God and Empire*. In it, as I recall, there is a statement very close to the one just quoted regarding God on Caesar's throne. I found the image troubling when I read *God and Empire* and I find it troubling now. The underlying religious or theological assumption is confounding. God on Caesar's throne?! Would whatever it is we call God actually "run the world" from Caesar's throne? There's theistic slight of hand here—unless Crossan intends the image as a playful joke, though I don't believe that's the case. If God is so theistically powerful as to run the world, why would God need Caesar's throne? Why doesn't God (if He needs or wants that throne) simply flick Caesar off it like the insignificant ant that Caesar presumably is? (This is no different than asking why God didn't prevent the Holocaust or keep the car from running over the child who wandered into the street—the sorts of questions that have been asked a million times.) Either God chooses not to exercise that awesome, total power or God has no such power.

I believe it's the latter. That's the first point. The second is the spiritual absurdity of imagining God on Caesar's throne running the world. Why would a God of power need Caesar's throne? Why would God do anything but repudiate a throne that represents the apex of a system of civilized exploitation and aristocratic oppression? How or why would God "run the world" through such a system when that imperial system is the antithesis of the kingdom of God? If the kingdom of God is about personal, communal, social, economic, and political transformation, transformation from the immanent, inside out, what's the relevance of depicting a conventional theistic, transcendent God running the world from Caesar's throne? What's the point?

Before he delves more deeply into the research of Solomon, Greenberg, and Pyszcynski, John Judis devotes a few paragraphs to social psychologists David Riesman, Christopher Lasch, and Ernest Becker, thinkers who operated "outside the academic discipline of psychology and were far more influenced by Freud and Marx than by B. F. Skinner and John B. Watson."[3] Judis quotes from Becker's *The Denial of Death*: "Man's anxiety results from the human paradox that man is an animal who is conscious of his animal limitation." And then Judis goes on to say that human beings "defend themselves against this fundamental anxiety by constructing cultures that promise symbolic or literal immortality." We practice "religions that promise immortality" and we seek to "submerge our own individuality in a larger, enduring community of race or nation." We "look to heroic leaders not only to fend off death, but to endow us with the courage to defy it." We also "react with hostility toward individuals and rival cultures that threaten to undermine the integrity of our own."[4]

Well, one of the intellectuals who has worked hardest (that I know of) to understand this "death grip" on the human mind, and to trace its development in human institutions, is Norman O. Brown. His book is *Life Against Death: The Psychoanalytical Meaning of History*. It is 322 pages of small print (in the underlined, dog-eared, battered paperback I've been rereading since 1974), wonderfully lucid, extremely well-written, and not exactly easy to summarize. I am therefore reluctant to try to condense Brown's argument. Instead, I will say the key concept for Brown is repression, and repression produces sublimation. Sublimation can be both idealization and deferment; and Brown somewhere says that, under conditions of civilization, sublimation is cumulative. It builds on itself and adds up.[II]

In the latter stages of Freud's thought, sublimation gets explicitly identified as the death instinct, death-in-life. As power structures accu-

II. Once again George Mosse provides us with a provocative image (on page 157 of his *Final Solution*) when he talks about how "the right penetrated so far down into the population through a mass organization." He is here describing a French anti-Semitic union, although I think it fair to say the Right in this country has had a similar penetration into the population especially since 1968. But looked at with E. J. Hobsbawm's particulars in mind—the extent to which the old ways of living were destroyed without the creation of a satisfactory substitute—and also bearing in mind the capacity of both church and state (and vested economic interests) to bend critical analysis toward a scapegoat outlet, we can begin to understand *why* virulent racism emerged in Europe when it did and *how* sublimation as idealization, deferment, and deflection evades critical self-analysis and builds toward explosive release. As ordinary people are unmoored from their authentic folk heritage (a process dreadfully compounded and made hugely more complicated by ideological fear of "the pagan" and religious hatred for "evolution") the professional AM radio demagogues and instant political celebrities hammer home the alleged linkage between government, socialism, feminism, homosexuality, environmentalism, and the Devil. The Right, in short, is in the business of hysterical agitation even as "liberals" are too ethically compromised and too economically habituated to imperial comfort to counter the Right's hysteria with thorough analysis and real conviction. Thus we drift toward wacky extremism and bizarre irrelevance even as global crises grow more ominous. Meanwhile, nearly everyone remains utterly in love with the moral, economic, political, and spiritual safety of civilization.

mulate more and more control (both in terms of institutional grip and outright lethality—i.e., "globalization" and "weapons of mass destruction"), death rules the world with increasing brazenness. Our personal acquiescence is very much a part of this process, for the flight-from-death impulse is deeply embedded in our religious understanding, in our culture, and in our personalities. (Perhaps this flight-from-death concept becomes less abstract and more grounded as we realize flight-from-death implies, at least in part, flight-from-nature, and our modern technological world can almost be defined as an accrued suppression and surpassing of nature.) So it is not insignificant that Brown, in his closing chapter ("The Resurrection of the Body"), turns most explicitly to Christianity with a question, a demand, and a plea:

> The path of sublimation, which mankind has religiously followed at least since the foundation of the first cities, is no way out of the human neurosis, but, on the contrary, leads to its aggravation. Psychoanalytical theory and the bitter facts of contemporary history suggest that mankind is reaching the end of this road. Psychoanalytical theory declares that the end of the road is the dominion of death-in-life. History has brought mankind to that pinnacle on which the total obliteration of mankind is at last a practical possibility. At this moment of history the friends of the life instinct must warn that the victory of death is by no means impossible; the malignant death instinct can unleash those hydrogen bombs. For if we discard our fond illusion that the human race has a privileged or providential status in the life of the universe, it seems plain that the malignant death instinct is a built-in guarantee that the human experiment, if it fails to attain its possible perfection, will cancel itself out, as the dinosaur experiment canceled itself out. But jeremiads are useless unless we can point to a better way. Therefore the question confronting mankind is the abolition of repression—in traditional Christian language, the resurrection of the body.
>
> We have already done what we could to extract from psychoanalytical theory a model of what the resurrected body would be like. The life instinct, or sexual instinct, demands activity of a kind that, in contrast to our current mode of activity, can only be called play. The life instinct also demands a union with others and with the world around us based not on anxiety and aggression but on narcissism and erotic exuberance.
>
> But the death instinct also demands satisfaction; as Hegel says in the *Phenomenology*, "The life and knowledge of God may doubt-

less be described as love playing with itself; but this idea sinks into triviality, if the seriousness, the pain, the patience and the labor of the Negative are omitted." The death instinct is reconciled with the life instinct only in a life which is not repressed, which leaves no "unlived lines" in the human body, the death instinct then being affirmed in a body which is willing to die. And, because the body is satisfied, the death instinct no longer drives it to change itself and make history, and therefore, as Christian theology divined, its activity is in eternity. . . .

If the question facing mankind is the abolition of repression, psychoanalysis is not the only point of view from which the question can and should be raised. We have already indicated that the question is intrinsic to Christian theology. The time has come to ask Christian theologians, especially the neo-orthodox, what they mean by the resurrection of the body and by eternal life. Is this a promise of immortality after death? In other words, is the psychological premise of Christianity the impossibility of reconciling life and death either in "this" world or the "next," so that flight from death—with all its morbid consequences—is our eternal fate in "this world" and in "the next"? . . .

In the last analysis Christian theology must either accept death as part of life or abandon the body. For two thousand years Christianity has kept alive the mystical hope of an ultimate victory of Life over Death, during a phase of human history when Life was at war with Death and hope could only be mystical. But if we are approaching the last days, Christian theology might ask itself whether it is only the religion of fallen humanity, or whether it might be asleep when the bridegroom comes.[5]

Lest we think "approaching the last days" only fanciful language, or "death-in-life" merely hysterical concept mongering, consider this analysis from Naomi Klein's "Disaster Capitalism" in the October 2007 *Harper's*:

After each new disaster, it's tempting to imagine that the loss of life and productivity will finally serve as a wake-up call, provoking the political class to launch some kind of "new New Deal." In fact, the opposite is taking place: disasters have become the preferred moments for advancing a vision of a ruthlessly divided world, one in which the very idea of a public sphere has no place at all. Call it disaster capitalism. Every time a new crisis hits—even when the crisis itself is the direct by-product of free-market ideology—the fear and disorientation that follow are harnessed for radical social and economic re-engineering. Each new shock is midwife to a new course of economic shock therapy. The end result is the same kind of unapologetic partition between the included and the excluded, the protected and the damned, that is on display in Baghdad. . . .

Given the boiling temperatures, both climatic and political, future disasters need not be cooked up in dark conspiracies. All indications are that if we simply stay the current course, they will keep coming with ever more ferocious intensity. Disaster generation can therefore be left to the market's invisible hand. This is one area in which it actually delivers.[6]

In other words, the very entity that epitomizes the tip of the civilized spear in the modern period—the ultradynamic capitalist economy—is the precise source of "disaster generation."[III]

If the death instinct sits on Caesar's throne, and if the kingdom of God represents the fullest possible transformation of human consciousness (from the deepest personal subjectivity to the most openly public of institutions), then the kingdom of God does not need Caesar's throne; and the idea or image of God on Caesar's throne is a fundamental obfuscation of both God and civilization. The image misrepresents both. It intimates a powerful God who inexplicably needs Caesar's throne, and it implies that Caesar's throne is in some way necessary or desired in order for the kingdom of God to be our preferred and actual political path.

The transformation of human consciousness inherent to the spiritual workings of the kingdom of God would not, of course, eliminate the need for governance. Human beings will always need to coordinate and manage, plan and respond. But such transformation would mean that God or the divine or Spirit is no longer *outside* the human body, but *within*. (Wherever else Spirit may be or move or inhabit.) Governance in the kingdom of God would be conducted by transformed human consciousness in councils of deep consideration and exhaustive dialogue. Its ethics would be based on what I've been calling radical servanthood and radical stewardship—decentralist democratic ecological socialism combined with vibrant plural cultures of rich local integrity deeply engaged with clean food, shelters built with local materials, alternative energy, local schools, modest healthcare facilities, inns, hostels, and cafes. It would not be based on systematic misrepresentations, half-truths, historical amnesia, outright

---

III. One hardly knows what to say when, less than a year after Naomi Klein's article appeared, the Wall Street implosion was immediately followed by massive federal bailouts for the imploders, while millions of people lost their jobs, savings, pensions, and homes.

lies, reflexive posturing, impulsive pandering, and high-velocity spin—or fixated on immortality.

Can we get there? Well, if Brown and Klein are right (I think they are), we are not yet done with globalized disaster in behalf of the malignant death instinct. Things are going to get worse. Therefore the danger of hydrogen bombs, for example, will not disappear until those bombs are dismantled. I believe transformation is possible even as I also believe that embracing transformation will be preceded by such a magnitude of shocks and suffering that human survival will literally teeter on the edge of the abyss before we awaken with stunned awareness. We will, as a species, confront what John Judis calls the "death grip." We will look death and extinction in the face, *and* we will be compelled to recognize that *we have done this to ourselves*, to the world, with our traumatic, civilized institutions in the service of the malignant death instinct.

This does not mean that death is our enemy. Far from it. From our place—our lives—on Earth, death is our inevitable destination. I am going to die. You are going to die. We cannot evade death except insofar as we participate in evasion mythologies, and they only serve to bring us back into the orbit of the malignant death instinct. If Spirit is capable of providing us or willing to provide us some life beyond death, we shall eventually discover what that life is. And if not, not. Getting through and beyond our anxiety about death is the task each of us has to face and achieve. This also involves letting go our fantasies of God as transcendent rescuer—or of imagining God on Caesar's throne, running the world. These are illusions that deter, restrain, disempower, and obstruct our requisite engagement with Spirit, with Earth, and with each other.

The kingdom is within us. If that's not true, or if it is insufficiently true, then doom in the guise of manic, ersatz immortality will overtake and crush us. As is implied in the temptation scenes of Jesus, the only god on Caesar's throne is the Devil—the embodiment of the malignant death instinct, the invisible hand of disaster, and the father of all political lies.

NOTES

1. Judis, "Death," 17.
2. Borg, *Heart*, 147.
3. Judis, "Death," 17.
4. Judis, "Death," 17, 18.
5. Brown, *Life*, 307–9.
6. Klein, "Disaster," 49, 58.

16

Restoring the Fundamental Assumptions

JUST AS I THOUGHT I was done with these polemics and provocations, two books showed up to goad my pen—*American Fascists: The Christian Right and the War on America* and *House of War: The Pentagon and the Disastrous Rise of American Power*. Both books are about fear—how fear fuels fascism, and how both greed and fear have shaped the nuclearized, permanent war economy and the military that is its brutal offspring.

As I recall from reading Brooks Adams' *The Law of Civilization and Decay*, fear and greed are represented as the two great underlying energies ruling human behavior and, thus, human history. Or, as Adams puts it:

> Thought is one of the manifestations of human energy, and among the earlier and simpler phases of thought, two stand conspicuous—Fear and Greed. Fear, which, by stimulating the imagination, creates a belief in an invisible world, and ultimately develops a priesthood; and Greed, which dissipates energy in war and trade.[1]

Perhaps—even including Pride, Lust, or sheer physical Hunger—no list of motives is exhaustive when it comes to examining or explaining human behavior. But remedy or cure for the global crisis may not depend on an absolutely ironclad final diagnosis. Physicians only help the body heal itself, although there are lots of people, so-called "conservatives" especially, who reject the idea that war can ever be curtailed because aggression is simply embedded in human behavior. Human nature will not change; war is a straightforward outgrowth of human nature; therefore war will always be with us. Secular "conservatives" simply say this is human nature, probably our ancient animal inheritance made increasingly complex and incrementally more deadly because of our inventive braininess. Religious fundamentalists promote the idea that "human nature" is flawed and distorted because of "original sin," but they also say there is no hope for change (except, perhaps, here and there isolated instances of personal change, due to religious conversion) until the End of Time. While some secular "conservatives" seem to actually revel in war—at least from the safe and comfortable distance as planners and cheerleaders—many fundamentalists believe war is how God fulfills His Plan, inscrutable as that may be to us, but always leading toward the tender and loving salvation of the elect. Because fundamentalists have such a brutally truncated perception of history, civilization does not have significance for them as a multimillennial "protection" racket new to history, while secular "conservatives" hold civilization in a place of exaltation precisely because it represents the victory of concentrated, elite will over common folk contentment and puts control in the hands of a focused and hawkish minority of the bold, bright, and capable. Fundamentalists have no critique of civilization other than Augustine's (and that tends toward theocracy), while "conservatives" invariably try to prune away as much "welfare" and "domestic" baggage as possible in favor or concentrated private wealth and ready executive power. And since these combined forces of "conservatives" and fundamentalists have brought us to our current global predicament, or at least they are now thrusting us heedlessly forward into that intensifying predicament, the great bulk of "liberal" doubt and hesitation about how to extricate ourselves from this increasingly dangerous trajectory is fraught with intellectual uncertainty and spiritual inadequacy. Therefore the "liberal" Left is invariably weak, timid, embarrassed, and compromising when not just caving in. This does not mean that "liberals" are worse human beings than "conservatives," only that our heritage, our institutions, and our outlook on life have been overwhelmingly shaped by Christian civilization (or civilized Christianity), and in the face of impending catastrophe and enlarging disaster we are stupendously lacking in deeper, alternative analyses and healing prescriptions. Where the Right gets to stand on an immense soapbox and shout about domination and superiority, the Left is reduced to blowing soapy bubbles of conciliation, compromise, and appeasement.

James Carroll relates how he went into his young son's room "to find him waking from a bad dream. He was crying. I sat with him, and when he could finally talk, he explained that, in his sleep, he had just been in China. He learned there that the Chinese have a word that, when uttered, makes it possible for parents to live forever. And then Pat's sobs overtook him again, as he wailed, 'But I can't remember what the word is.'" Carroll goes on to say:

> As I held my son, in the cold wash of my version of his fear, I un-
> derstood how our terrors were different. After all, in his dream life
> the Chinese were a source of wisdom, however elusive. In mine,
> beginning also in my youth, they were the enemy. My dread, that
> is, was attached to the ever-coming war, which was the permanent
> difference—fear of war being my patrimony—between my son
> and his father. My job in life has been the simple one of saying the
> word that will establish the reign of peace once and for all. This
> book was supposed to be that word. That word was supposed to
> restore the fundamental assumptions. That word, like Patrick's, was
> going to save us all. But by now it is clear again: I can't remember
> it either.[2]

James Carroll is a former priest who professes great regard for the Berrigan brothers Daniel and Philip. So it's a little stunning he can't remember the word that restores the fundamental assumptions. But that he says he can't remember is an interesting example of Christian amnesia. This amnesia virtually defines liberal Christianity's inability to grasp the radical nature of Gospel ethics. (George Lakoff, in his *Don't Think of an Elephant!*, says "One of the problems is that the progressive religious community, particularly progressive Christianity, doesn't really know how to express its own theology in a way that makes its politics clear, whereas conservative Christians do know the direct link between their theology and their politics. Conservative Christianity is a strict father religion."[3] Of course we need to remember that liberal theology, besides being retarded by the usual human evasiveness, is still struggling to find a new and fuller groundedness in a post-orthodox world, although a great many liberals seem to want to bring their comforting orthodoxy with them into the post-orthodox world.)

There's this wonderfully ironic scene in the opening of the movie *The Story of Vernon Johns*. In it, the new black preacher, brilliant and bold, has hitchhiked into an Alabama town and is sitting on a bench, with his paper bag of belongings beside him. Up drive three beautifully dressed black deacons who get out of the elegant car and begin looking for the preacher whom they walk right past and cannot see. Why can't they see him? Because he's not the sort of person they're looking for—as becomes abundantly clear as the movie progresses.[1]

Well, if we are locked into fear (with support from greed, pride, lust, and whatever other props or alternatives there are for fear), we are not inclined to recognize fear as our problem. The problem we see is the image projected by our fear: the communist, the terrorist, the Devil. We project our fear onto something or someone that's not us. (Or, as James Carroll puts it, evil "must be recognized as that which makes us think we are innocent of it."[4]) That the Christian Right should congeal as political fascism, and that the American experiment in democracy should ramify as globalized nuclear terrorism, proves that the opposite of what's expected can emerge from founding principles: fear and greed out of love and sharing, pathological superiority out of democratic equality.

We know what the words are, even if James Carroll says he can't remember. They are love, forgiveness, humility, nonviolence, and repentance. They (and others) can be shaped into wonderful social constructs, like the "kingdom of God." So it's not as if we don't know what to say. Acting stupid also protects our fear, greed, and pride—or, simply, our low-grade evasiveness. The meaning of Jesus on the cross is not that he magically atoned for our sins or was our substitute for enduring the wrath of God. The cross is a very public object lesson: this is what might happen *to you* if you mess with the power of the state, if you call into question its governing prerogatives, if you challenge the basis of the state's authority or propose its atrophy. (So when orthodox theology asserts that Jesus died on the cross so we don't have to, this simultaneously serves to disengage us from kingdom of God courage and to lift us into an otherworldly mental orbit.)

If it's the fear of death—including fear of the murderous power of the civilized state—that is the core impulse generating religions that promise immortality and political systems with heroic leaders in which we can submerge our individuality—I'm referring back to John Judis and his "Death Grip" article—then facing our mortality without escapist fantasy is to die to death. It is to be liberated from that fear—perhaps never fully liberated, but liberated sufficiently to recognize how fear is the hub of fascism, and liberated enough to not only desire the kingdom of God

I. For a lucid and factual account of Vernon Johns, see *Parting the Waters: America in the King Years 1954–63* by Taylor Branch, especially chapter 1 "Forerunner: Vernon Johns."

on Earth but to strive confidently for its realization, not only in terms of public policy but (perhaps even more difficult) also in the reconfiguration of our private lives. (How many of us feel publicly thwarted *and* privately blocked as we wrestle with frustration, bitterness, anger, and despair?) All that brings us right back to radical servanthood and radical stewardship, to the practice of practical, earnest leastness rather than the religious sanctimony and political aggression of presumed supremacy. We need to disarm our personal fear and private pride, lay down the weapons of war, and abandon all the exquisitely constructed layers of rationalization by which we evade the deliberate and intentional shaping of economic and political life according to the guiding principles of servanthood and stewardship.

"Democracy," says Chris Hedges in his final chapter "Apocalyptic Violence," "keeps religious faith in the private sphere, ensuring that all believers have an equal measure of protection and practice mutual toler-ance. Democracy sets no religious ideal. It simply ensures coexistence."[5] Later he excoriates "those who preach . . . grand, utopian visions" because "Dreams of a universal good create hells of persecution, suffering and slaughter."[6] The problem with the Christian Right, however, is not exactly its grand, utopian vision of universal good—and certainly not any *euto-pian* vision it may harbor. Its problem is pathological superiority, its con-viction of supremacy, its ridiculous literalism fenced with electric fear. We might even call it the Guantanamo Bay Syndrome. (Plus, for those in its midst who are sheer con artists, its brazen manipulative, megalomaniacal greed. And, for those who allow these con artists free rein, an absolutely stunning absence of spiritual discernment.)

It's not so much that Chris Hedges is totally wrong. In a world where religion reeks of contending hostile mythologies, keeping "faith" (or, more accurately, mythological literalism) in the private sphere can be politically prudent. But we are outgrowing that possibility, that option. The shoe no longer fits. We have outgrown containment and are now in the arena of confrontation. We really do need to ask what is so ugly and brutal about private religious conviction that its public manifestation results in perse-cution, suffering, and slaughter. Is Hedges implying a necessary quietistic powerlessness such as Ivan Illich advocated? Is spirituality so inherently otherworldly, so completely divorced from kingdom of God ethics, that only private powerlessness is capable of touching holiness? Is it either the-ocracy or cringing quietism? What we are facing—in Christian terms—is nothing less than the confrontation of Gospel versus Myth, the kingdom of God versus literalistic apocalypse. Nobody I know expresses this more acutely than Gil Bailie in *Violence Unveiled*. It won't do to try to shove the kingdom of God strictly into the private sphere or pretend it has no interest in public governance. If Bailie is right, the yeasty Gospel is a relentless, subversive fungus that intends to leaven the entire loaf of human conduct, most certainly including institutions of human governance, and it won't quit so long as there is material capable of being yeasted. (This also implies a slow, nearly imperceptible growth at first and, toward the end, a stunning, nearly miraculous culmination of unanticipated, even exponential speed.) Democracy may not set any religious ideal, but deeply ethical democracy is the necessary, logical, requisite outgrowth of Gospel yeast, of leastness, of a spiritual maturity that repudiates lording it over and dissolves supremacy's political justifications. Democracy is the soupy sponge in which Gospel yeast is making real bread. Democracy is a spiritual fungus. It is not spiritually neutral or "private."

Fascist, civilized theocracy versus libertarian democratic ecological socialism yeasted into being by radical servanthood and radical stewardship—that's the point we've begun to reach in the opening decades of the twenty-first century. But the elegance of our deflection from this realization is ancient and deep. In Book IV:34 in *The City of God*, Augustine says the Jews, if they had not killed Christ, would have kept their kingdom and been happier than Rome. Such is the foolishness of Platonic, scapegoating abstraction posing as visionary theology. And as the early, pious Thomas Merton says in his 1950 Introduction to *The City of God*, the book is a "summary of Christian dogma," the "autobiography of the Catholic Church," and the "secret of death and life, war and peace, hell and heaven."[7] If that is true, we are all well-dressed deacons walking right past a scruffy Jesus sitting on a park bench, contemplating us with a look of ironic amusement on his face—sizing up, yet again, the evasive and dense human material in which Spirit slowly works.

So once again I say—if there's no yeast, there'll be no bread, no wine. If Spirit is not yeasting us from within, our collective accrued falsity will surely do us in.

NOTES

1. Adams, *Law*, 6.
2. Carroll, *House*, 443, 444.
3. Lakoff, *Don't*, 102.
4. Carroll, *House*, 508.
5. Hedges, *American*, 196.
6. Hedges, *American*, 205.
7. Merton, "Introduction," x, xi, xv.

17

The Underbelly of the Superstructure

THE LOCAL LIBRARY RECENTLY obtained John Bowe's *Nobodies: Modern American Slave Labor and the Dark Side of the New Global Economy.* The book is mostly about the underbelly of American food production, about the "nobodies" who do the invisible gruntwork. Here are some rather impressive numbers that implicitly reveal to what extent underpaid farm workers help subsidize our food supply. From "1929 to 1958, Americans spent between 18 and 25 percent of their disposable income on food. From the mid-1980s to the present, the share has dropped, from about 12 percent to about 10 percent." In fact, says Bowe, "Americans in 2002 spent 6.5 percent of their income on food—less than any other country tracked. Canadians spent half again as much. Swedes spent nearly twice as much. Japanese spent over twice as much. Spaniards spent nearly three times as much."[1] Later, Bowe says:

> Current global-trade policies, however, led by American and European subsidy-driven food production, have resulted in food being sold abroad below cost, which in turn has forced dozens of millions of Third World peasants off their land. So as these hundreds of millions of people around the world have been "lifted" up from self-sustaining subsistence poverty, they have also been "lifted" off their land, "lifted" away from their extended families, "lifted" out of their traditional way of life, and herded into slums.[2]

Might we say these dozens or hundreds of millions of peasants have been "lifted" up into the underbelly of the superstructure, even as the superstructure itself overflows into squalid slums? Perhaps slums are, in fact, the superstructure's sagging underbelly. Here's Bowe again:

> At the time of the Western industrial revolution, the difference in per capita income between citizens of rich nations and those

of poor nations was negligible. In 2002, the difference was that people in the richest countries of the world earned approximately thirty thousand dollars per person per year, while those in the poorest earned about three hundred per year. To put it slightly differently, two hundred years ago, the income gap per capita between rich countries and poor ones was three to one. A hundred years ago, it had risen to ten to one. It currently stands at sixty to one and rising.[3]

Not enough numbers? Well, in his Introduction, Bowe says:

> Since 1970, the bottom 40 percent of American households lost an astounding 80 percent of their wealth. Currently, the top one percent of American households has gathered more wealth than the entire bottom 95 percent, and the richest 300,000 Americans pulled in as much income as the poorest 150 million. This is not wacko Internet stuff; these numbers are gleaned from the U.S. Bureau of Labor Statistics and the Census Bureau.
>
> The same trend of growing inequality is spreading all over the world. According to statistics from the World Bank, the number of people living on less than two dollars a day has risen by almost 50 percent since 1980, to 2.8 billion. In fifty-nine countries, average income is lower today than twenty years ago. The gap between the richest fifth of the world's population and the poorest fifth has doubled in the last fifty years. The top fifth has 80 percent of the world's income. The poorest fifth has one percent.[4]

Well, what's the connection between this trend toward growing inequality and food sold below the cost of production? Our government subsidizes corporate agribusiness. That means producers (large producers especially) can supply huge amounts of raw food commodities even though the prevailing market price is insufficient for the continuation of the production process. In other words, food is sold below the cost of production. And that means it's federal policy to depress food prices, which in turn means that small-scale producers the world over can't compete and can't survive, while farm workers are often hardly more than "free" slaves. Because so much agricultural production is now concentrated in so few agribusiness/corporate hands, this system of food production—created in large part by the steady strangulation of small-scale farming—has become "too big to fail." (If the collapse of "too big to fail" banks could plunge the country into economic chaos—perhaps, at least temporarily, a "chaos" like the utter quiet and tranquility of a city in the aftermath of a massive snow storm—collapse of energy-intensive and subsidy-dependent agribusiness would be a brutal Tough Love form of shock therapy for an obese nation hooked on corn syrup, sugar, and meat.) Bowe quotes former Supreme Court Justice Louis Brandeis: "We can have democracy in this country, or we can have great wealth concentrated in the hands of a few, but we can't have both."[5] I believe that's exactly true. I also believe the only way to reverse the trend toward aristocratic restoration is practical socialism combined with a massive reconstruction of small-scale agriculture, all of it within a democratic economy shaped and limited by ecological considerations.[1]

The ancient pattern of arrogant, rich aristocrat and subservient, destitute peasant will return with a vengeance (it's already well on its way, thanks in large part to capitalist individualism) unless we deepen our understanding of what democracy means. If it primarily means the Ayn Rand/William Graham Sumner view that a free man in a free democracy has no duty whatever toward other men, then democracy is dead in the water. Therefore the deepening of democratic consciousness depends on the spiritual recognition of servanthood and stewardship. But because the Christian churches have for centuries taught biblical literalism, a monarchical image of God, and reflexive obedience to authority, democracy is restrained from its necessary deepening by a kind of diffuse fear and political acquiescence inculcated by religious doctrine. (The long-standing alignment of the religious Right with the political Right shows where most religious people go when threatened or aroused.) So instead of Gospel ethics—the radical servanthood and radical stewardship within Jesus' kingdom of God proclamation—Christians have been taught political passivity and private holiness, although that doesn't prevent upsurges of anger and resentment, much of it channeled and even stoked by right-wing media agitators toward scapegoat outlets. The current crises in the world are to some immeasurable extent the consequences of Christian

---

I. In the 2008 Introduction to the new edition of his 1988 book *Family Farming*, Marty Strange, on page ix, not only tells us, with his genius for detail, that in the "past twenty years, farms in America have become much larger and food production much more concentrated," he also provides numbers: family farms declined by 29 percent in that period while farms with sales over $250,000 increased by 56 percent. "As a result of this consolidation, most food in America is now produced by a handful of mega-agribusinesses." See also my *Nature's Unruly Mob*, especially chapter 13 "Immeasurable Concepts" and chapter 16 "A Proper Balance."

orthodoxy's evasion of Gospel ethics. Christianity has not challenged empire so much as served as its cheerleader and bed partner.

It may seem dead wrong and even perverse to call the Christian Right "passive" when its arousal at the voting booth was a major factor in the election of George W. Bush—twice. And it may seem preposterous to say that world crises derive, at least in significant part, from Christianity's evasion of Gospel ethics. Yet these assertions are not only true, they are also intimately connected.

In his journal entry for Thursday, August 17, 1972, Bob Haldeman, Chief of Staff in the Nixon White House, reports a long conversation with evangelist Billy Graham, who had been operating as the go-between for Richard Nixon with both Lyndon Johnson and George Wallace. Haldeman says that Graham urged Nixon to "Hit the socialistic welfare state versus America where you can start at the bottom and work to the top. The only way the McGovern plan would work is under a dictatorship."[6] This linking of socialism to dictatorship, with its counterimage of heroic ascension from bottom to top, seems utterly normative in the evangelism industry—besides being in full contradiction to the Gospel injunction to be the least and servant to all, renouncing all inclination to "lord it over." Christians are therefore in an ethically vulnerable position, especially those who claim to be biblical literalists. There *is* no escaping the servanthood and stewardship demands of the Gospel; but by literalizing the *entire* Bible fundamentalists submerge the Gospel in a larger, more heroic epic of global salvation; and it is this larger mythological epic, including its "prophetic" trajectory toward world catastrophe, that has been (certainly since Constantine) the primary drive within Christianity and the rationale behind its alignment with political conquest.

This kind of Christianity has been wearing ideological blinders for centuries. (For those who don't know the word, "blinders" refers to the two leather flaps on a horse's bridle, positioned to shut out the side view and to keep the horse's attention ahead—what we might call induced tunnel vision.) Passivity is therefore associated with this forward-looking, narrowed vision. But it is also associated, in a troubled, unconscious way, with what the blinders obstruct. Christians who read the Bible can't help but be aware of and confronted by this ethical blind spot. But how to deal with it?

Well, obviously one of the ways to deal with the ethical blind spot is to slap it down with a politics that links socialism to dictatorship—

perhaps even invoking Stalin, thereby making socialism inherently atheistic and, therefore, evil and of the Devil, blithely gliding right over, for instance, the repeated presidential campaigns of socialist Norman Thomas,
a Presbyterian minister powerfully influenced by the social gospel as earlier propounded by Walter Rauschenbusch. So, unconsciously or subcon-
sciously, these nagging Gospel demands for leastness and servanthood,
blinkered by ideological salvationist blinders, contain a certain spiritual
energy needing not only articulation but integration into a larger conduct
of life. Christians, at some level, know this. But this knowing is largely
in the blinder zone, behind blinkered sight, and this nebulous knowing
mixes with an evangelistic politics that fiercely aligns socialism with Devil
dictatorship, so that leastness or servanthood can never be more than
private charity that helps move the believer toward personal holiness—
though works won't get you into heaven, and it is a sin to insist works will,
at least in some Protestant circles.

Is this knot complicated enough? You can't pray your way into heav-
en. You can't "good works" your way into heaven. You can't trick God or
slip past Him when He's not looking. So now what? Well, apparently fundamentalists say that adherence to the five "fundamentals"—the divinity
of Jesus, the virgin birth, Jesus' death on the cross as a substitute for our
sins, his physical resurrection and impending return, and the inerrancy
of scripture—concentrates your mind on the core cluster of necessary
beliefs that, taken together and wholly accepted, are tantamount to faith.
And since we are justified by faith, we've therefore made it through the
narrow door. We are *saved*. We've made a Eucharist of the fundamentals.[II]

Now once you know the truth, you must not stray from the narrow
path or you'll backslide and be lost. To stray is to fall into the snares of the
Devil, and those snares are all around us, though some appear benign and
oddly beckoning—like secular humanism or bleeding-heart liberalism or

---

II. Elaine Pagels, on page 129 of *Beyond Belief*, quotes from the second-century
church father Irenaeus in a polemic against gnostic heretics. In that polemic, Irenaeus
lists four of the five "fundamentals," leaving out only the inerrancy of scripture, although
it was a principle for which he was then fighting. I don't think it a stretch to suggest that
"fundamentalists" (the orthodox) won in their battle with "liberals" (the gnostics) prior to
Constantine (with Constantine sealing the deal), but that the restoration of that battle in
the modern period will conclude quite differently—even if (as Chris Hedges and others
prudently fear) Christian fascism my achieve temporary theocratic power in the coming
disruptions and breakdowns.

tree-hugging earthism. But they're not benign. They're snares of the Devil. So you must take care not to let the impulses of your heart overtake the guiding clarity of your head. (And, incidentally, since women have softer hearts, we men must diligently rule our wives and families with our harder heads.) "Passive" is therefore passive aggressive, a kind of fear-drenched state of spiritual blinkeredness whose inner stillness is a symptom of deep (but private and hidden) insecurity, whose aggression is directed against those whose behavior threatens the vigilant poise of this inner, insecure stillness. (And by "stillness" I don't mean tranquility or serenity but, rather, an all-seeing eye of anxious watchfulness, looking for the least little sign of Devil infiltration.) How else to explain a "Christian" country with Earth-destroying nuclear weapons whose dominant religious mission is to set the stage and establish the preconditions for Armageddon? What is this but a monumental case of blinkered spiritual passive aggressiveness that stands ready to usher Earth into holocaust? A pious suicide cult. The death instinct infiltrated into religious ideology as a blinkered posture of holy obedience.

We need to go back to yeast, to the smallest of seeds, to leastness and servanthood. If the Gospel is true—in the sense of its relentlessly bubbling ethical qualities—then Gospel will enable us to transform human governance from monarchical fear to servanthood friendliness, from spear to pruning hook, from nuclear bomb to solar panel, from aristocratic presumption to the stewardship of libertarian democratic ecological socialism. Separation of church and state is, if not the wrong argument, at least a minor or diversionary argument. The right argument has to do with Christians embracing the Gospel, trusting Spirit, and entering into the peace—including the political peace—that passes all understanding.

We are closing in on the last stage of our exodus story, our wandering in the civilized wilderness, our standing on the threshold of the eutopian Promised Land. We can't go into the Promised Land with weapons, with our hatreds and fears, our exploitative economic systems, or our hubristic, Creation-wrecking ideology of Progress. Or, as Jean-Pierre Dupuy puts it in the epigraph that opens these essays, "either the inauguration of the Kingdom of Love or else a destructive apocalypse for which we will have only ourselves to blame." The only way we can get to the Kingdom of Love is by disarming, by making ourselves vulnerable, by embracing the other, by consenting to economic sharing and lifestyle simplicity, by renewed ecological reverence for Creation. It's either that or we'll blow the place to hell. Either we trust in Spirit (whose next mythic embodiment will be the Daughter) or Earth will wallow in disaster. If it's the latter, the deepening of democracy is moot. But if it's the former, we will discover an incredibly rich, earthy groundedness precisely as we learn to live with humble Gospel ethics, as we let go of and repent of our idolatrous, blinkered Myth.

In *The Last Battle*, the final book in C. S. Lewis's Chronicles of Narnia, the dwarfs have already been thrust through the stable, out of Narnia and into The Great Land Beyond. But they are stubbornly suspicious. They sit in a xenophobic circle, on the grass, holding hands, letting no one in, exhorting each other to keep their eyes tightly closed, squeezed shut, for fear they might see something beautiful and be tricked. It's a brilliant image every child can understand.

The dwarfs are us. We are the dwarfs. The kingdom of God is here. It has arrived. We are in it. Its beauty is all around us. All we need do is open our ridiculously fearful eyes and stubbornly constricted hearts, and let the sun shine in.

NOTES

1. Bowe, *Nobodies*, 52.
2. Bowe, *Nobodies*, 272–73.
3. Bowe, *Nobodies*, 272.
4. Bowe, *Nobodies*, xvi.
5. Bowe, *Nobodies*, xvi.
6. Haldeman, *Haldeman*, 495.

18

Something of a Watershed

HENRY STEELE COMMAGER, IN his 1950 book *The American Mind: An Interpretation of American Thought and Character Since the 1880's*, says the 1890s constitute "something of a watershed" in American history.[1] This was, more or less, the crucial decade that contained the political defeat of rural, agrarian America and the victory of urban, industrial America. Rural America, especially in the central area, in the Midwest, was both religious and radical. Yet the People's Party, the party of agrarian populism, projected all manner of socialist ideas in its platform. It was the historical basis for the New Deal forty years later.

In 2004, Thomas Frank's *What's the Matter with Kansas?* was published as an inquiry into "how conservatives won the heart of America," in the words of the book's subtitle. Frank's entire book, lucid and witty, is a puzzled, anguished investigation into how right-wing "populism" of present-day working-class America promotes the exact opposite political and economic platform than that advocated by prairie Populists of the late nineteenth century. Present-day "populism" seeks to undo the lingering provisions and programs of the New Deal. As Frank says,

> ... conservatives love populism in theory, always imagining super-authentic working people as witnesses to nature's endorsement of their privileges .... From Fox News and the Hoover Institute and every newspaper in the land they sing the praises of the working man's red-state virtues even while they pummel the working man's economic chances with outsourcing, new overtime rules, lousy health insurance, and coercive new management techniques.[2]

He goes on to say that conservatism's considerable power "is its airtight explanation of reality, its ability to make sense of the average person's disgruntlement while exempting laissez-faire capitalism from any culpability."[3] (He also says "The deafness of the conservative rank and file to the patent insincerity of their leaders is one of the true cultural marvels of the Great Backlash."[4]) The question begging an answer is How can people lack so much discernment? How can early twenty-first century "populists" have almost exactly the opposite economic convictions of their late nineteenth-century ancestors? How did the weathervane of spiritual discernment—political understanding is derivative from spiritual discernment—shift one-hundred eighty degrees in a century? The only possible conclusions are that the fundamentalism of nineteenth-century populism was far more deeply rooted in Gospel ethics than present-day fundamentalism and that the social psychology contained within small-scale agrarian culture was hugely more grounded than the social psychology produced by an alienated and bewildered consumerism. Nineteenth-century populists were people who had not yet made a complete transition to industrial alienation in that process described so succinctly by E. J. Hobsbawm.

Commager, in his final chapter "The Twentieth-Century American," especially in parts 3, 4, and 5, provides some implicit answers to Frank's questions, even as those answers seem to address symptoms rather than root causes. Specifically, Commager puts the finger on advertising as it both firmed up and shaped a rapidly changing class consciousness:

> The most convincing evidence of class consciousness was to be found in advertisements. Advertisers, who presumably knew what they were about, appealed more and more to the snob instinct. They celebrated not the virtues of their product but the social distinction of those who bought it, and keeping up with the Joneses was abandoned for the more titillating task of keeping up with the Biddles. It was supposed to be a guarantee of the merits of a tobacco or a liquor that it appealed to those whose names could be found in the Social Register, while the merits of Mozart and Beethoven were enhanced by the approval of ladies and gentlemen who habitually dressed for dinner.
>
> Along with and not unconnected with class consciousness went what seemed a steady decline of taste. Democracy, here, seemed a matter of leveling down rather than up. Vulgarization could be read in the newspapers, the magazines, the comics, and in much that passed for literature; it could be seen in the moving pictures and heard on the radio. It could be discovered, above all, in advertisements which, during the second quarter of the century, reached the nadir of vulgarity.

American society, as popular advertisements portrayed it, was a nightmare of fear and jealousy, gossip and slander, envy and ambition, greed and lust, where almost any means were justified to attain private and selfish ends, where sentiment was meretricious, ideals tarnished, and virtue debauched. The typical American, as they pictured him, lived in a torment of anxiety and cupidity and regulated his conduct entirely by ulterior considerations. He read books to make conversation, listened to music to establish his social position, chose his clothes for the impression they would make on business associates, entertained his friends in order to get ahead, held the respect of his children and the affection of his wife by continuous bribery. To the advertisers nothing was sacred and nothing private: they levied impartially upon filial devotion, marriage, religion, health, and cleanliness. Love, as they portrayed it, was purely competitive: it went to those who could afford the most lavish gifts and was retained only by incessant attention to externals. Friendship, too, was for sale: to serve inferior liquors or confess to shabby furniture was to forfeit it. Advancement came not through industry, intelligence, or integrity, or any of the old-fashioned virtues but was won by an astute combination of deception, bribery, and blackmail.

All this presented to the student of the American character a most perplexing problem. It was the business of the advertisers to know that character, and their resources enabled them to enlist in its study the aid of the most perspicacious sociologists and psychologists. Yet if their analysis was correct, the American people were decadent and depraved. No other evidence supported this conclusion. Advertisers appealed to fear, snobbery, and self-indulgence, yet no one familiar with the American character would maintain that these were indeed its predominant motivations, and statesmen who knew the American people appealed to higher motives, and not in vain. The problem remained a fascinating one, for if it was clear that the advertisers libeled the American character, it was equally clear that Americans tolerated and even rewarded those who libeled them.[5]

Now it may be that Commager is more encyclopedic than deep and so fails to plumb the depths he's revealed. Plus, the "leveling down rather than up" imagery obfuscates the essential dynamic: that manufactured commodities packaged in images of imitation aristocratic elegance were extinguishing folk production and transforming folk consciousness into commercial mass consensus. "Democracy" is only political cover for what is, at heart, an utter transformation from self-provisioning folk culture to commercially saturated mass consumerism. This is much less a "leveling down" than a fake escalation of cultural taste. Ernest Becker says "the degradation of commercial advertising is a logical and coherent part of a particular kind of world view," and that commercial society "actually is subverting the whole individual by reducing him to a role-playing part."[6] Commager's observation that the "American people were decadent and depraved," if looked at through the filter of advertisements, certainly suggests the decadence and depravity of the filter itself and, behind it, the economic system whose core energy was and remains a relentless aristocratic drivenness empowered by essentially religious convictions of refined civility overpowering and obliterating all forms of backwardness and all residues of primitivity. Isn't Commager implicitly saying that as the old rural culture of self-sufficiency was crumbling, as life became increasingly saturated with manufactured commodities (with their virtually ubiquitous commercial imagery), elite corporate interests utilized the brightest manipulative techniques of the Seven Deadly Sins not merely to sell a vast array of products and establish a permanent market (though that was certainly the goal), but to mock and ridicule the old culture of self-sufficiency and substitute for it not merely new products but an entirely new set of standardized attitudes and mass perceptions?

So the answer to the question How can people be so oblivious? seems to be: this is what happens to folk consciousness when its cultural container is destroyed and an ideology of endless consumer progress is commercially substituted, an ideology of consumerism packaged, when necessary, in virulent empire patriotism in which corporate interests are hidden, disguised, but paramount. I cannot help but believe that this is precisely what Jurgen Habermas had in mind when (according to Arthur McGovern) the economic base becomes a function of government activity, when that base is taken up into the superstructure. Now throw into this mess the reality of globalization, with its worldwide condemnation of backwardness, its weapons of ecocidal lethality, resource limitation, population growth, burgeoning energy consumption, the global grab for oil and natural gas, extinctions, climate change, and varieties of fervent religiosity with divine imperialism, and is it any wonder there's something the matter with Kansas? Here's how Jared Diamond puts it in his *Collapse*:

People in the Third World aspire to First World living standards. They develop that aspiration through watching television, seeing advertisements for First World consumer products sold in their countries, and observing First World visitors to their countries. Even in the most remote villages and refugee camps today, people know about the outside world. Third World citizens are encouraged in that aspiration by First World and United Nations development agencies which hold out to them the prospect of achieving their dream if they will only adopt the right policies, like balancing their national budgets, investing in education and infrastructure, and so on.

But no one at the U.N. or in First World governments is willing to acknowledge the dream's impossibility: the unsustainability of a world in which the Third World's large population were to reach and maintain current First World living standards. It is impossible for the First World to resolve that dilemma by blocking the Third World's efforts to catch up: South Korea, Malaysia, Singapore, Hong Kong, Taiwan, and Mauritius have already succeeded or are close to success; China and India are progressing rapidly by their own efforts; and the 15 rich Western European countries making up the European Union have just extended Union membership to 10 poorer countries of Eastern Europe, in effect thereby pledging to help those 10 countries catch up. Even if the human populations of the Third World did not exist, it would be impossible for the First World alone to maintain its present course, because it is not in a steady state but is depleting its own resources as well as those imported from the Third World. At present, it is untenable politically for First World leaders to propose to their own citizens that they lower their living standards, as measured by lower resource consumption and waste production rates. What will happen when it finally dawns on all those people in the Third World that current First World standards are unreachable for them, and that the First World refuses to abandon those standards for itself?[7]

Or, as Thomas Frank asks:

Why shouldn't our culture just get worse and worse, if making it worse will only cause the people who worsen it to grow wealthier and wealthier? ... [Y]ou can't help but wonder how much farther it's all going to go.... How much more of the "garden of the world" will we abandon to sterility and decay?

My guess is, quite a bit.... And even if the state must sacrifice it all—its cities and its industry, its farms and its small towns, all its thoughts and its doings—the brilliance of the mirage will not fade. Kansas is ready to lead us singing into the apocalypse.[8]

However, lest we pick unnecessarily on Thomas Frank's poor, hapless home state of Kansas, allow me to relate last evening's discussion at our weekly Peace Study. One of our members—Tom—had been to Georgia the weekend before Thanksgiving to participate in the annual protest against the School of the Americas, the Pentagon-sponsored "school of the assassins" that has trained thousands of Latin American soldiers in "counterinsurgency" techniques. Tom brought back several videos, a couple of which we watched. The discussion that followed had to do with the possibility of showing one or more of those videos to local church groups. The Catholic among us said she could arrange a special showing at her church, probably through the Peace and Justice Committee, but nobody would come. The Lutheran said (it's the Missouri Synod she attends, not the ELCA) she would have to ask permission; she was sure the pastors would say no; no point even to ask. The woman from the United Church of Christ said she could maybe get away with showing a video at a Mission Committee, especially the video about helping wounded kids from Iraq, but references to "illegal war" made the video "political" and the church is "absolutely petrified" of losing its tax-exempt status. (My wife Susanna and I kept quiet, so as not to rub it in; but everybody knew we attend Friends Meeting, and there's not a video in the bunch we couldn't take and show. Such is the freedom when ecclesiastical authority and rigid doctrine are not permitted to own, drive, and manage the spiritual vehicle.)

Well, this morning I flipped on Wisconsin Public Radio and there, on an early talk show, was discussion of last night's Republican presidential-candidate debate in Florida. The host of the talk show played a snippet of a question to Mike Huckabee about the death penalty—specifically, What would Jesus do? Huckabee, in reply, went on and on about how he attended to each and every execution order that passed his desk as Governor of Arkansas. But these were heinous crimes, he said, the inmates were all guilty, and society has a right to execute for reasons of deterrence. (No hint in Huckabee's answer that the system might in any way be flawed, biased, or based on class, race, or revenge.)

When Huckabee was done, the moderator said, "You didn't answer the question: What would *Jesus* do?"

"Jesus," replied Huckabee, "was too smart to run for public office." That remark, said the WPR talk-show host, got the "biggest laugh" of the night. Jesus, you see, is always and everywhere totally above politics, and wasn't Mike Huckabee so very quick and witty to point out that obvious and traditional truth. Ha, ha; case closed.

In the December 10, 2007, issue of *The Nation*, Chris Hedges has a passionate piece entitled "Hands Off Iran." And in the Fall 2007 issue of *The Catholic Peace Voice*, editor Dave Robinson ticks off the factors that could just make the U.S. invasion of Iran a "perfect storm." Hedges' image is that this "neat little war . . . has the potential to ignite an inferno." Plus it could result in "the death of the Republic."[9] He's dead serious.

I see no need at this point to itemize the particulars of these two honest, searing pleas beyond noting that Hedges says an attack on Iran would "ignite the Middle East."[10] For nearly two years I have been predicting that it's hard to imagine Bush and Cheney leaving office without having first attacked Iran—and, even more cunning, to calculate the timing of that attack so as to give as big a boost to the Republican presidential candidate as is possible. Not too soon, not too late. Just enough "patriotic" fear and fervor to tip the election in the Republican direction.[1]

People like Bush and Cheney had to deeply *believe* some things in order to act (as they did) with relentless, seemingly tireless consistency in behalf of willful executive power. Those beliefs can't have been, strictly speaking, based on greed because both Bush and Cheney are wealthy men, and they couldn't possibly be worried about ending up on skid row. Their beliefs must therefore have to do with power, with control, with vindictive righteousness, with an obsessive desire to transform the entire world into a certain image of holiness, of cleansed goodness, of evil vanquished. Theirs was a project of stupendous labor and monumental hubris.

There are only two cosmic candidates big enough for this magnitude of hubris, only two metaphysical entities sufficiently sovereign to wear such massively justifying combat boots. One is God. The other is Civilization—though perhaps the latter should be qualified as *Western* Civilization. Of course, God and Civilization are sacred beings living within the temple of our fear, awe, and adulation. Both God and Civilization are inherently superlative. Madness is not a term permitted in such sacred precincts. What's inside the temple is *super*, above and beyond any piddling earthly

I. Obviously, that attack did not occur, and McCain lost the election. But is it only my reluctance to admit I was wrong to say that it might well have been the economic meltdown, in the fall of 2008, that kept Bush from such an attack and McCain from victory?

consideration, *above* our puling analysis, *far beyond* our nibbling little critiques. The goodness of God and the greatness of Civilization are transcendent and therefore beyond prosaic criticism.

Now patriotism may be a mixture consisting of 73 percent Civilization and 27 percent God (I am making up these numbers, these proportions, out of my imagination), but a patriot worships *pater*, and *pater* is the Father. And so the new holocaust of violent righteousness is presenting a holy gift to *pater*, a burnt offering of evil bodies, all in the bottomless yearning to be loved by God, embraced by God, sanctified and made holy by God, and ultimately rewarded by God for single-minded moral devotion. This is the righteous madness we have arrived at, the confluence of globalized civilizational power with a religious mythology of supreme certainty, last days, and end times. Politically, with apocalyptic lethality, it is not necessary for the practitioners of global holocaust to stick rigidly to one or the other of these interwoven streams. It may not be possible to do so anyway, for Religious Myth and Civilizational Myth have in many ways merged, having flooded over any mere theoretical "wall of separation." The temporary and provisional separation of church and state has been breeched. It's a done deal, at least since the early nineteenth-century announcement of Manifest Destiny. That's what Thomas Frank doesn't quite see. Supremacy has alternating current.

That's why I say the crisis we are in is something of an epochal culmination. It's not just another normal cosmic crisis. This one has been caused by the utter wreckage of the folk cultures that were foundational to all prior cultural evolution, leaving Earth vulnerable to the ravages of civilized, utopian hubris. This one is a pivot that could also be a radioactive period. Or an aristocratic restoration. Or the unfolding of the kingdom of God into a Daughter's age rich with Gospel ethics, servanthood and stewardship transformed from abstract spirituality into practical politics. The kingdom of God is Green—decentralist, ecological, libertarian, ecological, and socialist. Its spirituality is feminine. Its antithesis is desolation.

NOTES

1. Commager, *American*, viii.
2. Frank, *What's*, 151.
3. Frank, *What's*, 162.
4. Frank, *What's*, 235.
5. Commager, *American*, 416–17.
6. Becker, *Structure*, 274, 273.
7. Diamond, *Collapse*, 495–96.
8. Frank, *What's*, 250–51.
9. Hedges, "Hands," 6, 4.
10. Hedges, "Hands," 4.

19

Prophets Raging in the Slums

MANY OF THE BOOKS I read come from the local library, for which institution I am truly grateful. I also browse the racks at favorite thrift stores, Salvation Army and St. Vincent de Paul especially—or, as they're called in the local vernacular, Sally Ann and Saint Vinnie's. Recently at one of these stores I found Tony Allan's *Prophecies: 4,000 Years of Prophets, Visionaries and Predictions.* It's something of a coffee table book. *Prophecies* includes a chapter on the "Calendrical Systems of Mesoamerica" with its explication of the Mayan calendar that comes to an end on December 21, 2012. There is also a chapter on Joachim of Fiore ("The Apostle of the Third Age") and another ("The Papal Predictions") on the "so-called prophecies of St. Malachy," the priest who introduced the Cistercian order to Ireland. We have already touched on Joachim, with his invocation of Three Ages, which I have enlarged to Four Ages. Malachy did something else. He provided a list of characteristics for all future popes.[1] Malachy's list ends with the pope who will follow the current pope, Benedict. Here are Malachy's words describing who many believe will be the last pope: "In the last persecution of the Holy Roman Church there shall reign Peter the Roman, who will feed the sheep amid great tribulations; and when these are passed, the city of the seven hills will be utterly destroyed and the terrible judge will judge the people."[1]

Prophecy, says Allan in his Introduction, is less about prognostication than it is the bearing of a divine message, although the "idea of the future insinuated itself into the prophets' armory, and in time it became its most important component, making the very word 'prophetic' synony-

---

1. See also Martin Lings' "Saint Malachy's Prophecy," pages 83 through 89, in the Spring 1996 issue of *Parabola.*

mous with 'prescient' or 'predictive.'"[2] However, in Michael Birkel's *A Near Sympathy: The Timeless Quaker Wisdom of John Woolman*, we find that:

> The prophets served as models, not only of how those who are faithful to God among an unfaithful people can expect to be rejected and despised by their own community, but also as models of interior purification. They set aside their own predispositions in order to conform to the will of God. Having purified their motives, they were granted a clear understanding of God's desires for human society, namely, that people must exercise true justice and righteousness. The writings of the prophets and those of John Woolman are laden with the terms "justice" and "righteousness"—and so we see that John Woolman is also indebted to the prophets for the content of his call to reform. Yet the process of inward purification that led to insight into the nature of justice and righteousness was often a painful one.[3]

So what does it mean to set aside our own predispositions, have our motives purified, and be granted a clear understanding of the divine desire for human society? Abraham Heschel, in the opening chapter ("What Manner of Man is the Prophet?") of his book *The Prophets*, says:

> A student of philosophy who turns from the discourses of the great metaphysicians to the orations of the prophets may feel as if he were going from the realm of the sublime to an area of trivialities. Instead of dealing with the timeless issues of being and becoming, of matter and form, of definitions and demonstrations, he is thrown into orations about widows and orphans, about the corruption of judges and the affairs of the market place. Instead of showing us a way through the elegant mansions of the mind, the prophets take us to the slums. The world is a proud place, full of beauty, but the prophets are scandalized, and rave as if the whole world were a slum. They make much ado about paltry things, lavishing excessive language upon trifling subjects. . . . Why such immoderate excitement? Why such intense indignation? . . .
>
> The prophet is a man who feels fiercely. God has thrust a burden upon his soul, and he is bowed and stunned at man's fierce greed. Frightful is the agony of man; no human voice can convey its full terror. Prophecy is the voice that God has lent to the silent agony, a voice to the plundered poor, to the profaned riches of the world. It is a form of living, a crossing point of God and man. God is raging in the prophet's words.[4]

It seems that even as we celebrate "prophets"—invariably old, dead, venerated, and harmless, or, like Nostradamus, glaring fiercely up at us from the cover of the *National Enquirer*—we are rather oblivious of the prophets in our midst, perhaps like Naomi Klein. Part of the problem (but only part) is that we tend to piously conflate prophet not only with the predictive, but also with a very conventional image of God. We can't seem to imagine a "prophet" without the traditional invocation of God or without that "prophet" being associated, in some way, with a conventional image of God. That may be, at least in part, why we don't recognize Lewis Mumford and Norman O. Brown as major prophets in the latter half of the twentieth century. These men, in ways that overlap, looked deeply into human history and into the dynamics of human behavior, set aside their own predispositions, had their motives purified, and were granted a clear understanding of Spirit's desire for human society. At least I believe that's one way to explain their insightful brilliance.

Did Brown and Mumford believe in God? Did they believe God was raging in their words? Had either of them been asked such questions, I suspect they would immediately have wanted to know what the questioner meant by "God" and "believe." And if they would have been asked whether their predispositions had been set aside and their motives purified, they may have been interested in what the questioner did or did not believe about the doctrine of original sin or whether human nature was unchangingly warlike. Prophets, in other words, are unlikely to be comfortable as objects of our gushing (or even quietly pious) veneration.

The difficulty, however, with being optimistic about any imminent unfolding of Spirit's desire for human society (whose unfolding desire we might rephrase as the kingdom of God or the Age of the Daughter) is the extent to which our lives are governed by forces that are antithetical to the kingdom of God, certainly including forces that may have aggressively appropriated the language of the kingdom of God but whose politics—like Thomas Frank's contemporary "populists"—are all about asserting empire. (Frank talks about "social conservatives who raise their voices in praise of Jesus but cast their votes to exalt Caesar."[5])

It's a little inexplicable how some people just seem prophetically trustworthy. For instance, I heard former U.S. Marine and one-time U.N. Weapons Inspector Scott Ritter on Wisconsin Public Radio on the eve of Bush's invasion of Iraq in March 2003. Ritter said, with what seemed to me great authority, there are no operable weapons of mass destruction in Iraq and (this stunned me) the US will lose the war. The first quickly showed itself to be true, and the second is taking a little longer to unfold. So maybe we should go back to Chris Hedges and Dave Robinson, whose specifics in regard to Iran I chose not to quote earlier. If their utterances might not be precisely predictive, they certainly are prescient. That is, the alarm that Hedges and Robinson raise comes from their prophetic sensibility. Here's Hedges from his "Hands Off Iran":

> A war with Iran is doomed. It will be no more successful than the Israeli air strikes on Lebanon in 2006, which failed to break Hezbollah and united most Lebanese behind that militant group. The Israeli bombing did not pacify four million Lebanese. What will happen when we begin to pound a country of 65 million people whose land mass is three times the size of France?
>
> Once you begin an air campaign it is only a matter of time before you have to put troops on the ground or accept defeat, as the Israelis had to do in Lebanon. And if we begin dropping bunker busters and cruise missiles on Iran, this is the choice that must be faced: either send US forces into Iran to fight a protracted and futile guerrilla war, or walk away in humiliation.
>
> But more ominous, an attack on Iran will ignite the Middle East. The loss of Iranian oil, coupled with possible Silkworm missile attack by Iran against oil tankers in the Persian Gulf, could send the price of oil soaring to somewhere around $200 a barrel. The effect on the domestic and world economy will be devastating, very possibly triggering a global recession. The Middle East has two-thirds of the world's proven petroleum reserves and nearly half its natural gas. A disruption in the supply will be felt immediately.
>
> This attack will be interpreted by many Shiites in the Middle East as a religious war. The two million Shiites in Saudi Arabia (heavily concentrated in the oil-rich Eastern Province), the Shiite majority in Iraq and the Shiite communities in Bahrain, Pakistan, and Turkey could turn in rage on us and our dwindling allies. We could see a combination of increased terrorist attacks, including on American soil, and widespread sabotage of oil production in the Persian Gulf. Iraq, as bad as it looks now, will become a death pit for US troops. The Supreme Islamic Iraqi Council, which has so far not joined the insurgency, has strong ties to Iran. It could begin full-scale guerrilla resistance, possibly uniting for the first time with Sunnis against the occupation. Iran, in retaliation, will fire its missiles, some with a range of 1,100 miles, at US installations, including Baghdad's Green Zone. Expect substantial casual-

ties, especially with Iranian agents and their Iraqi allies calling in precise coordinates. Iranian missiles could be launched at Israel. The Strait of Hormuz, which is the corridor for 20 percent of the world's oil supply, will become treacherous, perhaps unnavigable. Chinese-supplied antiship missiles, mines and coastal artillery, along with speedboats packed with explosives and suicide bombers, will target US shipping, along with Saudi oil production and oil export centers.

Hezbollah forces in southern Lebanon, closely allied with Iran, may in solidarity fire rockets into northern Israel. Israel, already struck by missiles from Tehran, could then carry out retaliatory raids against both Lebanon and Iran. Pakistan, with its huge Shiite minority, will become even more unstable. . . . The neat little war with Iran, which many Democrats do not oppose, has the potential to ignite an inferno.[6]

And here's Dave Robinson with "The Perfect Storm":

We are witnessing the gathering of all the elements to produce a perfect storm: A pair of religiously-fundamentalist presidents who share a messianic sense of their own place in history; a powerful, recklessly hawkish Vice-President whose only intelligible agenda is a single-minded service to the international oil and gas industry; a likely low-intensity conflict already underway with U.S. special forces killing Iranians in Iran and Iranian proxy forces killing U.S. soldiers in Iraq; accusations of the development of nuclear weapons by Iran and the threatened use of nuclear weapons by the U.S.; a foreign policy for hardliners in Israel and their lobbyists in the U.S.; a weak and acquiescent U.S. Congress; and a looming election. This is the making of a true killer storm. . . .

President Bush . . . is under tremendous pressure from both Israel and Vice-President Cheney to move against Iran militarily before relinquishing the White House to what, in all likelihood, will be a Democratic successor. . . .

Meanwhile, the U.S. has engaged in a new strategy of arming and supporting Sunni militias in Anbar Province in Iraq. These militias are at the center of the insurgency against the Shiite government in Baghdad—which the U.S. previously cleared the way for through its invasion, occupation and the rushed election process. That Shiite government is dominated by members of the Supreme Council for the Islamic Revolution in Iraq (SCIRI), who, until the U.S. invasion, were exiles hosted in Iran. The Iranians have longstanding ties with SCIRI and they continue to receive support from Tehran.

Indeed, the ties between Iraq and Iran are much deeper than most of the U.S. public knows. More than a million Iranian pilgrims visited Iraq last year. Iraq does more than a billion dollars in trade with Iran annually....

For Israel's right-wing Likud government, the destruction of the Islamic regime in Iran is of the highest priority. Israeli leaders went along enthusiastically with the Bush Administration's plan to invade Iraq, even though they were pressing harder for military action first against Iran—the last military threat to Israel in the region. The power of the pro-war wing of the Israeli lobby in the U.S. Congress is unmatched....

And then there is our Vice-President. Alan Greenspan's admission that the Iraq war "was largely about oil" is an affirmation of our pre-war attempts to counter the bogus claims about weapons of mass destruction which the Administration used to obscure the true motivations for its invasion. Iran, like Iraq, sits on huge oil deposits. In addition, Iran sits on 50% of the world's natural gas reserves.... If the U.S. went to war in Iraq for oil and that effort has led to the death of 1.2 million Iraqis, it is clear that Vice-President Cheney will not be deterred by the possibility of another million or more deaths in Iran when the prize there is even greater.

One would think that the gaggle of Democratic contenders for the White House would be at the forefront of challenging this Administration's new march to war with Iran. Not so. Instead, many Democrats have chosen to use Iran as a whipping boy in order to court voters and appear to be strong on defense as a means of mitigating their so-called opposition to continuing to fight in Iraq....

Huge oil and gas reserves, Israeli geopolitical priorities, Iranian involvement in Iraq, a Congress too weak to exercise leadership, an Iranian president who is easily demonized, and a U.S. President with a messianic and personalized worldview. This is a perfect storm.[7]

What's obvious here is that this issue—the possible bombing and invasion of Iran—has serious Middle Eastern implications and would generate world repercussions. Prophecy, says Tony Allan, "is a psychological necessity for humankind."[8] I suppose that means we can't help thinking about the future and meditating on how things could be different than they are. This "psychological necessity" can, I think, also help explain why so much public hope and expectation is invested in and lavished on political stars, as in Barack Obama's campaign and election in 2008. Jonathan Schell, seriously disappointed with Obama's first year in office, nevertheless urges the president to "Ally himself more passionately, more eloquently with the real" and to "Give voice even to unpopular truths."[9] Schell goes on to say "There is a power in the real that it is going untapped. It is the power of that salubrious, galvanizing, irreversible inner shock that you feel when the veil falls from your eyes and the truth of something is placed before you."[10] (A grimly cautionary position regarding "The March of Folly," however—Barbara Tuchman's 1984 book on disastrous governmental policy "From Troy to Vietnam"—suggests that overcoming persistence in error is "the most repugnant option in government."[11] Or, as she goes on to say, "For a chief of state, admitting error is almost out of the question."[12] But Tuchman can't help, on her last page, holding out the hope of "moral courage."[13]) Perhaps the uniqueness of Barack Obama is that he really does seem to recognize the need for moral courage and the necessity to give voice to unpopular truths. But we have yet to see whether he will risk the prophetic voice of moral courage or, with flashes of lofty rhetoric to the contrary, continue to slide smoothly down the well-traveled path of folly.

To get to the real stuff, however, we need people such as John Woolman who have, perhaps, set aside their own predispositions, voluntarily entered into a process of interior purification, and are ready for a clear understanding of Spirit's desire for human society. It's either repentance or disaster. That much is clear. That's where we're at. Either interior purification or externalizing disaster promotion. What's the matter with Kansas is what's the matter with America and, to varying degrees, what's the matter with the entire world. Civilization as an organizing principle based on murder, coercion, hubris, and theft is locked into externalization, into what George Orwell apparently called "protective stupidity."[14] These characteristics lie in civilization's origin and they have continued on as civilization's historic legacy, just under the gilding of cultural superiority and spiritual triumphalism. (It's certainly not incidental that the biblical prophets arose *after* Israel became a monarchy and began to fulfill the dire warnings recorded in I Samuel 8, predictions having to do with the imposition of slavery arising from the nature of the monarchy itself.)

When Henry Steele Commager, Ernest Becker, and Jarad Diamond mull over the meaning of commercial advertising and see the unreachable, untenable, and unsustainable implications of induced commodity lust, the lesson to be grasped in the commercialization and globalization of civilization is that *civilization has been and is inherently unsustainable*, especially as it has become industrialized and as its ersatz aristocratic standard of living has become "democratic." Its globalization disrupts both the cultural coherence and the ecological integrity of the entire planet. This may well be one of the hardest lessons for us to accept, in part because we have been taught by no less a foundational authority than Augustine that:

> The cause, then, of the greatness of the Roman empire is neither fortuitous nor fatal, according to the judgment or opinion of those who call those things *fortuitous* which either have no causes, or such causes as do not proceed from some intelligible order, and those things *fatal* which happen independently of the will of God and man, by the necessity of a certain *order*. In a word, human kingdoms are established by divine providence.[15]

But in Matthew 4:1–10 we have a very different story. These are the temptation scenes of Jesus in the desert. In the third temptation, the Devil has taken Jesus

> . . . to a very high mountain and showed Him all the kingdoms of the world and their splendor, saying to Him, "All these I will give You if You will kneel and worship me." Then Jesus said to him, "Begone, Satan; for it is written, 'You shall worship the Lord your God and serve Him alone.'"

(In Luke 4:6–7, the Devil says "All this authority and the splendor of them will I give You, for it has been handed over to me and I bestow it on whomever I please; so if You will worship me, it shall all be Yours.")

I am not proposing belief in a cosmic good-versus-evil struggle between God and the Devil, as is the stock in trade of fundamentalist evangelism. I am pointing to something far more mundane, something explicitly historical: that the organizing principle of civilization is made up of violent, elite, aristocratic, unsustainable greed packaged in fantasies of world-ordering omnipotence backed by a stage effect of heavily gilded divine mythology. It may be that no one in the West exceeds Augustine as gilder-in-chief. No one has done more to link empire to God's will. Therefore the shedding of this mythology is not simply a matter of setting the record straight by means of secular scholarship, of coming to terms with the facts of history, or even of hoping for a president with moral courage—but also and more deeply letting go of the traditional melding of human kingdoms and divine providence, a melding that has deeply penetrated our operative assumptions about the nature of reality. This conventional melding is by no means confined to fundamentalism, for it underlies the bulk of all Christian teaching since Augustine, harkens back to Romans 13, and can even be found in John 19:11. There Jesus tells Pilate, "You have no power whatever of your own, but only what is granted you from above"—one of those Fourth Gospel otherworldly remarks that aligns so easily with Romans 13 and Augustine's view of kingdoms and empire, but is the antithesis of I Samuel 8.

We need—the world needs—an organizing principle based on compassion, helpfulness, humility, and generosity. In Christian teaching, that organizing principle is the "kingdom of God," as articulated explicitly in Matthew, Mark, and Luke. It's time to quit arguing about whether this "kingdom" is possible on Earth. It's time to commit ourselves to the interior purification (if that's what it takes) that just might make this "kingdom" possible. But first we have to want it, believe in its possibility, and stop obstructing its growth because we cling with more conviction to "realist" historians and pious theologians who tell us why this "kingdom" is impossible than to the historical Jesus who simply set about making it happen.

NOTES

1. Allan, *Prophecies*, 37.

2. Allan, *Prophecies*, 6.

3. Birkel, *Near*, 49.

4. Heschel, *Prophets*, 3, 5.

5. Frank, *What's*, 178.

6. Hedges, "Hands," 4, 6.

7. Robinson, "Perfect," 3.

8. Allan, *Prophecies*, 7.

9. Schell, "Understanding," 23.

10. Schell, "Understanding," 24.

11. Tuchman, *March*, 383.

12. Tuchman, *March*, 384.

13. Tuchman, *March*, 387.

14. Tuchman, *March*, 384.

15. Augustine, *City*, 142–43.

20

Legitimating the Policeman

IS THIS REALLY THE last word? We'll see.

In a way, we'll let Daniel Callahan have the last word or at least—with his close companions Sigmund Freud and Philip Rieff—ask the final question. In his second chapter, "Pathologies of Civilized Communities" in *The Tyranny of Survival*, Callahan says it is

> . . . exceedingly difficult to see how Freud's analysis of the tension between individual and civilization can lead to anything other than an ethic of social repression with survival as the dominating value. By casting the individual and society as antagonists, the ground is laid for legitimating the policeman as the final symbol of cultural unity and preservation; "law and order" quite properly becomes the dominating slogan and political fact of life, with "freedom" the enemy as soon as it endangers good order and "justice" the weapon with which each is repressed in the name of all.[1]

Callahan also says that "Freud himself leaves open the possibility that, if nothing really new has been introduced into the society of man, the very fact that society is now more advanced than ever, more 'civilized,' means that the power of destruction, aggression and death have been intensified."[2]

In chapter 5, "The Tyranny of Individualism," Callahan devotes himself to Philip Rieff's explication of Freud:

> In the struggle between Eros and Thanatos, Freud saw the drive of Eros leading to an ever-widening scope of relationships; Eros seeks greater unity and human bonding. Biologically, then, the impetus of the life principle is not entirely in the direction of an individualistic satisfaction of instinctual urges—so much at any rate Freud argued in *Beyond the Pleasure Principle* and in *Civilization and Its Discontents*. The movement toward greater unity, entail-

ing progress forward in the face of the backward-pulling power of Thanatos and toward a cumulatively greater range of relationships, is envisioned as a life principle because it nullifies the essence of the death principle—which destroys relationships and seeks a return to an original state of isolation and stasis. Rieff sees no evidence that any such power is now at work. "We are," he writes, "privileged to be participant observers of another great experiment by Western humanity upon itself: an attempt to build upon the obsolescence of both love and hatred as organizing modes of personality." There is indeed a tyranny, dressed up in a fresh new gown, but proclaiming as ever the obsolescence of what we have always known.

The irony with which Rieff analyzes psychological man makes evident his distrust and final rejection. But Rieff offers little to put in its place, in great part because he does not offer a positive view of culture which would strike a good bargain between the demands of the individual and of the culture. No more than Freud can he offer the foundation for a social ethic which would integrate a range of values in a way that would enable the individual and civilization to mutually behave toward each other in ways which respected the requirements of each. What Rieff has done is to lay bare the *hubris* and folly of an individualism run amuck, seeking a final break from all cultural restraints.[3]

Now it has to be said that Callahan rather contemptuously dismisses Norman O. Brown, Lewis Mumford, Theodore Roszak, and Jacques Ellul (the latter three are merely "preachers against technology," writers whose books "make provocative bedtime reading,"[4] while Brown "has nothing to offer but a regression to nothingness"[5]). Callahan also betrays a rather stunning intellectual arrogance that is implicitly revealed in his lack of distinction between "culture" and "civilization." (Nowhere does he even remotely define his terms.) All of that constitutes a serious deficiency in discernment. How are we to believe what he says if he won't say what he means? And yet, for all that failing, the idea from Freud that "nothing really new has been introduced into the society of man," and from Rieff that there is "no evidence that any such power"—a life principle of greater unity—"is now at work"—those assertions cannot be easily evaded or simply ignored. Certainly the political aftermath of 9/11 has underscored the impulse toward legitimating the policeman, for a colossal heightening of global conflict ("civilization versus terrorism"), and for a truly frightening upsurge in religious apocalypticism with its lustful anticipation of world carnage.

So—is there really nothing new in human society? No evidence of any greater unity now at work?

If Freud and Rieff are correct, if the answer is no—nothing new, no evidence of greater unity—then my hope is without merit, without a basis other than wishful thinking, something worthless and possibly even worse than worthless. But nothing new also means no Spirit is bubbling in the human soul, and that Gospel-as-yeast is only a cute literary concept devoid of psychospiritual substance. It also means that my modified Joachimism, with its anticipation of the Daughter, is pure concept mongering. And, finally, it means there's no escape from a rapidly accelerating and intensifying global carnage brought about by the deadly combination of civilized arrogance and willful religious blindness. Religious fanatics will prove themselves magnificently correct, at least in the arena of disaster. The doctrine of original sin will have achieved its "theological" victory—though we shall have to wait to see (*if* we get to see) whether redemption and final salvation come to true believers. Perhaps we'll just all be dead. Maybe God, in absolute and total disgust, will transfer the entire human experiment to the DoD—the Department of the Devil—with a one-way ticket to Hell.

But, if my hunch is correct, the kingdom of God is far more subtle and infiltrating than creed-hardened theologians and hidebound ecclesiastical authorities have suspected—or, if they have suspected it, it is a suspicion that smelled to them either of sulphur or of compost. Spirit continues to bubble within; Gospel does have devious properties of transformative yeast; and Joachim's three-age configuration is true but incomplete. (So it's not Father, Son, and Holy Ghost, but Mother, Father, Son, and Daughter.)

However, witty (or witless) insouciance on my part does not prove my point of view. People can, and do, say all sorts of things with apparent deep conviction, things not worth the paper they're printed on. So, do I finally *know* what I'm saying is true? Yes and no. I *know* that love *is* the great healing salve, and I *know* that servanthood and stewardship *are* the ethical principles we absolutely need to guide us into a culturally rich and ecologically conservative Green future. But do I *know* if Spirit is strong enough to overcome our mythological hubris? No, I don't—for the crucial test will not come via supernatural intervention but by our willingness (or unwillingness) to let go of our protective mythology and stand vulnerable in the ethics of nonviolent servanthood and reverent stewardship. But we must not underestimate the power of pride, contempt, and unacknowledged anxiety, or of fear posing as "realism." And that is also why I've written these polemics and provocations. If anything I've said can help tip the scale in the direction of the kingdom of God I will have done my duty in and toward Creation. What else am I to do or say? I love life too much, as Thoreau says in his essay "Civil Disobedience," to cast my vote as a "strip of paper merely," and not with my "whole influence," such as that influence may be.[6] As Thoreau goes on to say:

> The best thing a man can do for his culture when he is rich is to endeavor to carry out those schemes which he entertained when he was poor. Christ answered the Herodians according to their condition. "Show me the tribute-money," said he;—and one took a penny out of his pocket;—if you use money which has the image of Caesar on it and which he has made current and valuable, that is, *if you are men of the State,* and gladly enjoy the advantages of Caesar's government, then pay him back some of his own when he demands it. "Render therefore to Caesar that which is Caesar's, and to God those things which are God's,"—leaving them no wiser than before as to which was which; for they did not wish to know.[7]

We have not wished to know which is which. But such not-knowing is now globally fatal. Waking up to how we vote—a strip of paper for Caesar or our whole influence for Spirit—is therefore the most pressing life-decision at hand. There is no evading this registration in the polling place of Creation.

NOTES

1. Callahan, *Tyranny*, 31.
2. Callahan, *Tyranny*, 24.
3. Callahan, *Tyranny*, 133–34.
4. Callahan, *Tyranny*, 260.
5. Callahan, *Tyranny*, xi.
6. Thoreau, "Civil," 292.
7. Thoreau, "Civil," 293.

21

An Unseemly Eulogy for My Father

As we in my father's immediate family were facing his ambiguously imminent death, we began—perhaps with a little guilt—to think and talk about his funeral. I say "ambiguously imminent" because, at 96, he was a tough old knot, and just when we thought he was done for, or nearly so, he'd stabilize and begin talking about "recovery." It felt, you know, a little unseemly to be discussing the funeral of a man still living and, in some respects, very much alive. But we also knew that plans must be considered before the fact, as it were, or else the entire event would be swept along by professional management. And if there was one thing Otto Henry Gilk was sure to balk at and resist, it was professional management.

He told my wife Susanna he did not want a church funeral. He also did not want (as he put it) a "feed." We intend to overrule him about the feed, because funerals are not only about respecting the wishes of the dead but also about sharing a meal with those still living. A funeral can also be an occasion for reflecting on the life of the person who's died— memories, aggravations perhaps, unfinished thoughts and unconcluded conversations. Whether this is "closure" or just slipping in the last word is open to debate.

Anyway, we decided to strike a compromise with my father's wishes in regard to a funeral. That is, we decided on a home wake or visitation, during which time people could come to pay their respects, as the saying is, and then hold a more focused memorial service, after burial, organized but hopefully relaxed and informal, during which people could speak and say what was on their hearts and minds.

Henry was a talker, as everybody who knew him knows. He was never a great listener—except, perhaps, while listening for deer in the woods— but as he got older and more deaf, his listening, such as it was, got worse. Thin conversation was replaced with bursts of monologue. Those around him were sometimes buried under his stories and the tireless reiteration of his religious convictions. He rarely asked what it was *you* thought. He was too busy remembering the Great Depression of the 1930s or asserting what he believed the Bible really said.

His stories *were* interesting, even though he told them too often and never seemed to realize his listeners were numb with excess verbiage. Fewer stories carefully told would have kept the villagers returning to the pump with empty buckets, instead of bailing out their swamped basements while looking desperately for the stairwell. Henry did, after all, live through a huge cultural transformation, and his best stories (there *were* a great many) reveal the rural folk life of an America not yet fully industrialized, a life in which woodburning cook stoves, a cow or two, a flock of chickens, a tired old horse, and a huge annual garden were as typical as a DVD, a microwave, or the internet are today.

It's not my intention or desire to repeat stories now.[1] I want to do something else. I want to respond to my father's religious convictions, to have, perhaps, a small slice of conversation I never really had with him when he was more capable of such conversation. A funeral, after all, is supposed to address some of the deeper and more elusive questions of life—like "Who am I?" or "What's the meaning of all this commotion?" or "What happens to this 'me' when I die?" Because he often prayed out loud—and really quite loud, given his deafness—I knew he repeatedly asked to be taken directly to heaven and given a job to do, not so much complaining to God about the silly, wasted effort and unnecessary expense of having his body buried in a box, as puzzling over why such ridiculous rigmarole was required if, in the end, he was to be lifted out of that box anyway, on the occasion of the general resurrection. Getting buried in a coffin, inside a cement vault, even if dressed in flannel shirt and bib overalls, all of it placed underground in dirt, after a potentially boring, pious, and obsequious funeral process, just didn't sit well with an old farmer who had his bib overalls washed and took a bath once a week, at most. This might become a rather tough talk.

First, I want to recognize the obvious: Henry *had* religious convictions. He had them, I believe, before he became a Seventh-Day Adventist, somewhere around 1970. But his affiliation with the SDA really put

---

I. Henry's stories, supposedly well-edited, are being prepared by an elusive scarecrow of the northwoods named C. D. (Seedy) Buckberry. Apparently Resource Publications, the catchall imprint of Wipf and Stock, has taken on this project!

a lock on those convictions and made them more like a fist—or so it seemed, anyway, to those of us on the outside. Second, I need to repeat that part of the difficulty in conversing with Henry about religion was that he wasn't particularly skilled in the arts of conversation, especially the listening aspects. Conversation, for him, mostly meant telling stories. But another part of the difficulty was that he *had* convictions *and* he had read the Bible to back up those convictions. Many of us—including myself—did *not* have firm convictions and we had *not* read the Bible or any other book of spiritual wisdom with devoted single-mindedness. We might have dabbled with or piddled in "spiritual wisdom," but our hearts weren't in the effort. So not only was conversation burdened by Henry's unlistening convictions, it was also weak on our end because, quite simply, we didn't know what we believed—or, alternatively, our beliefs were in the process of major change and basic reformulation, and we weren't prepared to articulate or defend them. We felt at a disadvantage. Having entered into a process of theistic decomposition, wittingly or unwittingly, those of us in the charnel house of God's putrefaction felt an impossible disconnect between the litter and debris of rotting divinity and the bland, blaring, and seemingly lucid certainties of a biblical literalism larded with apocalyptic anticipations. And so our main impulse, as Henry climbed up on his soapbox of convictions, was to terminate the conversation—insofar as it was a conversation—and to do so as quickly as possible. This, of course, disturbed him. In other words, lots of things were never threshed out. I might even say lots of things festered. Henry's preachiness became a point of aggravation and resentment, and our turning away was, I'm sure, emotionally agitating for him. He wanted to see us *saved*, or at least have a crack at it, and we were not cooperating. It must be a tough thing to believe that your own sons are on a stubborn, willful, and blind path to hell.

Now there are various ways to examine this situation. From Henry's point of view the truth was obvious, as plain as the nose on your face. The Bible, for him, was the inerrant Word of God, and nowhere can you find in it any authorization by God for switching the sabbath from Saturday to Sunday, from the seventh day of the week to the first day of the week. Sure, Jesus rose from the dead on the first day of the week, but the Bible doesn't therefore switch Sabbath observation from Saturday to Sunday. So all Sunday Christians were merely following the "doctrines of men," the lawyerly rationalizations of early Christian schemers, and, by so doing, were disobeying God and, probably, dooming themselves to the Hot Spot in the next world.

I don't believe I ever argued the sabbath point with Henry. Why not? Because I considered it a subsidiary matter. By disputing the sabbath, we weren't getting down to brass tacks. So what are the brass tacks? Well, my father would often say that the ancient Catholic church had selected Sunday to be the new "sabbath" specifically to distinguish itself from the Jewish synagogue. He also said the Protestant churches, from the Reformation onward, had continued with Sunday as "sabbath" because they weren't adequately Bible-based, even though Martin Luther had apparently asserted that the foundation of the church was *sola scriptura* or "by scripture alone." That is, by scripture alone were Christians to grasp the meaning of the Christian faith—as opposed, for instance, to the "apostolic succession" the Vatican boasted of.

I didn't dispute any of this. The early church *did* obviously switch from Saturday to Sunday, and the great bulk of Protestant denominations continued with Sunday worship. That's obviously true. What I did, or at least what I tried to do, was to ask him why he accepted seventeenth-century astronomy but not twentieth-century astronomy.

So why is that in any way important? Well, in 1633 the famous astronomer Galileo was arrested by Catholic authorities and threatened with torture unless he recanted his assertion that Earth revolved around the sun. The Bible, you see, supposedly said the sun goes around Earth, not Earth around the sun, and so Galileo's astronomical observations simply had to be false. They were heretical. The Catholic church at that point believed in the inerrancy of scripture—or, if not exactly inerrancy in the manner that later fundamentalists would insist upon, then in the authenticity and certitude of church doctrine and teaching. Therefore Galileo was wrong and had to be wrong. Therefore his false teaching had to be suppressed lest it corrupt susceptible minds and lead people astray.

My father, however, was taught at the Copper School, out in the Town of Harding, in northern Wisconsin, in the 1920s, that Earth goes around the sun. Once a year. That's what astronomers say a year is—one complete circuit of Earth around the sun. To my knowledge, my father never doubted Galileo's truth as taught in the Copper School. He may have said "sunrise" and "sunset," as we all do, but he believed that Earth goes around the sun, and not the other way around. His acceptance of astronomical truth, however—not to speak of geological truth, or botanical truth, or zoological truth, or anthropological truth, or archeological truth, stopped dead in its tracks by the time it got to the nineteenth century, for these latter truths asserted an ancientness of time and an evolution of life that contradicted the six-day account of Creation in Genesis. If science had discovered and was speaking truth, then Genesis as a supposedly factual account of the origin and process of Creation was *not* factually true. Here was the brass tack. And, since my father believed in *sola scriptura* and the inerrancy of the Bible, he was compelled by his religious convictions to reject these sciences (what he knew or had heard of them) as false teaching. Now, of course, he didn't carefully examine the evidence and come to his own measured rejection; instead, his rejection flowed automatically from his a priori religious conviction: if the Bible was literally true in its most basic stories, science was full of hot air. That's all there was to it. That's all you needed to know.[II]

Perhaps this is the point at which to clarify the term "fundamentalist." Somewhere around 1895, a bunch of so-called "conservative" Christians got together and, in an effort to refute and deny a big hunk of modern "liberal" science (especially those parts of science exploring the ancientness of Earth, the solar system, and the universe, plus of course, anything remotely smacking of "evolution"), said there were five basic "fundamentals" a real, true Christian had to believe. These five were and are: the divinity of Jesus, the virgin birth, Jesus' death on the cross as a substitute for our sins, Jesus' physical resurrection and impending return, and (the one that not only glued them all together but implicitly asserted factual truth out of all basic Bible stories) the inerrancy of scripture.[III]

II. On page 34 of his *Technopoly: The Surrender of Culture to Technology*, Neil Postman says that "Copernicus, Kepler, and Galileo put in place the dynamite that would blow up the theology and metaphysics of the medieval world. Newton lit the fuse. In the ensuing explosion, Aristotle's animism was destroyed, along with almost everything else in his *Physics*. Scripture lost much of its authority. Theology, once the Queen of the Sciences, was now reduced to the status of Court Jester." We can of course say that the current Court Jester is embodied by the wacky Right—wacky, perhaps, like Charlie Chaplin's film mockery of Hitler but also as potentially dangerous as the Fuhrer himself. We can also say (thinking of Postman's subtitle) that if the fundamentalism of nineteenth-century American populism was a struggle *against* the surrender of culture to technology (as well as to capitalism), the present brand of fundamentalist "populism" is far less culturally grounded, given to emotional hysteria and political Manicheanism, and devoid of any substantial intellectual critique of either technology or capitalism.

III. In *The Story of Christianity: The Reformation to the Present Day*: Justo L. Gonzalez provides, on page 257, a brief summation of what he calls "the anti-liberal reaction that

I never heard my father use the word "fundamentalist." I don't hon-
estly know if he thought he was one. But I believe he was. And so I would
say to him, when he slipped into his SDA excursions, "The premise on
which your entire argument rests is the inerrancy of scripture. But since
the time of Galileo, the inerrancy of scripture has been shown to be a
fiction. That is, the inerrancy of scripture is a false teaching. And if we say
that God is Truth, then the inerrancy of scripture is not a truth emanating
from God but, rather,"—and this was a choker—"a doctrine of men." To
assert to him that *sola scriptura* was a "doctrine of men" was to plug his
cannon with mud and dare him to light the fuse.

At this point, I would say, my father always and consistently practiced
pure evasion. The argument I put up against his threatened the foundation (and therefore the entire edifice) of his worldview. It was scientific
discovery versus a doctrine of scriptural inerrancy. It was a threat he
handled by retreating back behind the Bible. Or, more accurately, it was
a threat he handled by retreating behind a doctrine of biblical inerrancy.
Our conversation had nowhere to go.

As far as I could ever tell, my father's notion of who and what God is
was dependent on accepting core Bible stories as literally and historically
true. The six-day Creation was true. Cain killing Abel was true. Noah and
the flood was true. Moses parting the Red Sea was true. True in the sense
that all these stories were literally and historically factual. They really happened. For my father, God was pretty well locked up in the doctrine of
biblical literalism. Lacking a deeper knowledge of history, isolated from
penetrating intellectual analysis, and almost totally unfamiliar with rigorous academic scholarship, he turned toward apocalyptic religion for an
explanation of how the world worked, of what its destiny was. This drift

---

came to be called 'fundamentalism.'" He also says that the fundamentalist "emphasis on
biblical inerrancy and its rejection of many of the conclusions of biblical scholars made
it possible to juxtapose texts from different books of Scripture, and thus to develop a
number of schemes outlining and explaining God's actions, past, present, and future."
My father's Adventism was chock-full of such juxtapositions, with a virtual underground
railroad running between the books of Daniel and Revelation.

But Gonzalez also describes, on pages 253 and 254, how similar mainstream "conservative" and "liberal" Christianity were in America in the late nineteenth century—racist,
civilized, and ultra-Protestant. In these ways, American Protestant Christianity was very
much like the European Protestant Christianity George Mosse describes in his chapter
"Infected Christianity" in his *Toward the Final Solution*. This is not meant, however, to
overlook the part Catholicism has played in these political disasters with its own brand of
supremacy, nor to suggest that genuine conservative thought leads invariably to fascism.

towards biblical apocalypse was truly tragic because the religious mode he eventually embraced was one of the most fundamentalist of all fundamentalisms. He became a Seventh-Day Adventist. By doing so, he locked himself into a biblical literalism (the world was created only five or six thousand years ago) that prevented him from grasping or even considering a bigger and more complex picture. He couldn't bring himself to see how gatherers developed horticulture eight or ten thousand years ago because, finally, it was downright wicked to think that human history was shaped in other ways than Eve persuading Adam to bite the forbidden fruit, their eviction from the Garden of Eden, or Cain doing in Abel. Like fundamentalists everywhere, my father substituted religious mythology for the hard, sometimes painful work of examining real history, and he pushed away real history (unless it was about the American West, but even then it had a thread of Zane Gray romanticism in it) because fundamentalists have to believe real history is a kind of wickedness offered temptingly and seductively by the Devil. That's the process, for religious fundamentalists, whereby truth is evil—a box outside of which the wickedly untrue waits to snare its prey. And, I'm sorry to say, my father, with his eighth-grade education and lack of exposure to a larger intellectuality, fell into the fundamentalist trap of biblical literalism. He became a true believer. That also meant (in his view) there was "nothin' you kin do about it." That is, the Big Struggle was between God and the Devil, and the best a person could hope for was to understand the truth of the Bible, cling mightily to it, and hope to be chosen by God, on Judgment Day, for inclusion into Heaven, rather than be sent, with the goats, to Hell.

Politics, in this mode of understanding, was useless, foolish, and a waste of time. (Because they disagreed so—fundamentally, I suppose—with Sunday fundamentalists over the question of "sabbath," many Adventists held back from overt political alignment with the mainstream Christian Right. Adventists like my father feared that Sunday fundamentalists, if they could achieve their theocratic objectives, would make Sunday worship mandatory, thus institutionalizing in civilized law heretical disobedience to God's Law.) Besides, the world is about to end. So even if (in theory) politics could do something useful and creative, the time was short, Christ was coming, and getting right with God and the Bible was what everybody needed to do: let go of your "doctrines of men" and cling with all your might and main to the True Word of God. And, because he had read the Bible with such diligence and care (though, of course, he did scriptural picking and choosing, as everyone does), he *knew* or *thought* he knew, what the real Word of God was.

There wasn't a lot of wiggle room in this formulation. And it is this stubborn blindness that corporate America has tapped into, largely via AM radio demagogues like Rush Limbaugh and Sean Hannity, in order to constantly agitate the working class against all those damned stupid foolish ungrounded elitist *liberals* who seem to believe in one goofy theory after another. That is, the people who own and run Big Business in America are not sufficiently numerous to elect their preferred candidates to high public office. In this effort, they need lots of electoral help, lots of votes, from people who are fairly poor. And they've been getting those votes—for Richard Nixon, Ronald Reagan, Bush I, and Bush II—from so-called "conservative" Christians who love their religious and nationalistic mythology more than they love the hard, humble truth, and who are even willing to vote against their economic interests in order to (supposedly) support "traditional values." Meanwhile, the truly wealthy laugh all the way to the bank.

It seems that the huge divide between so-called "conservative" Christians and so-called "liberal" Christians has to do overwhelmingly with their respective images of God. For the most part, "conservative" Christians are also fundamentalists, or at least literalists to some degree. This, then, seems to be the process by which so-called "conservative" Christians come to their image of God: they do so in a way directly analogous to set design in a theater. I don't mean this sarcastically, not in the least. I mean to simply be descriptive. I mean that the *stories* we all were taught—that God created everything in six days, that Lot's wife got turned into a pillar of salt, that Noah built an Ark that contained a pair of all animals, that Jonah got swallowed by a whale, that Moses parted the Red Sea with his staff—are the scenery, the set design, *through which* we "see" the main hidden character. That main character is God. God is both playwright *and* (hidden) actor. The stories provide the means through which we "see" a God of tremendous strength and awesome power. These *stories* were taught to us as true history. That is, we were told the stories were historically factual. They actually happened. Therefore God is the Person described.

But the net impact of science and hard-nosed historical scholarship has been to discredit these stories as actual history and to render them metaphorical or symbolic stories from which, if we're able, we can find spiritual insight. So-called "liberals" have been journeying down this metaphorical path. But (here's the point) to go down this metaphorical path is to be faced with the dissolution, the decomposition, of the traditional image of God. It's not just a matter of letting go of the biblical "scenery." It's also a letting go of the image of God the traditional scenery projects. In my estimation, this is the pivot point between so-called "conservatives" and "liberals."

Now in the public fight that's been going on with increasing virulence for a few decades, "conservatives" accuse "liberals" of abandoning God, of moral relativism, of atheism, and of no longer being truly Christian. "Liberals" often don't know what to say in reply to this verbal assault because, having let go of an image of God they no longer find credible or believable, it's not simple or easy to come up with a new, better, fuller, or more apt image. To stick just a moment longer with the theater construct, "conservatives" continue to cling to the traditional scenery while "liberals" are stumbling around backstage in darkness and clutter. "Liberals" are waiting for a new inspiration, a new revelation, a new and deeper understanding, but "conservatives" claim to already have the inspiration, the revelation, the old and deep understanding. Within this dynamic, "conservatives" have largely dominated American politics, for what we call "conservative" and "liberal" in the realm of politics largely derives from or at least correlates to what "conservative" and "liberal" mean in the religious sphere. Since at least the presidency of Richard Nixon, "conservatives" have become fiercely assertive about the "truth" they know is true, while "liberals" have entered into what medieval theologians called "the dark night of the soul."

In this "conservative"/"liberal" split, I personally was raised in a thoroughly "conservative" atmosphere but began to enter a long "liberal" dark night of the soul before I was twenty years old. This internal struggle went on in me for over two decades. With the collapse of my third (!) marriage in 1988, I came to the painful conclusion that I needed to be more serious about spiritual clarity and spiritual healing. Since my upbringing was in the mainstream Protestant tradition, and since "Christ" is the formal title given to a Jewish peasant named Jesus, I decided to try and find out what the teachings of Jesus had to tell me. I was licking my wounds.

Very quickly I found I couldn't read, or didn't want to read, the letters of Paul the Apostle. I didn't want anyone, including Paul, interpreting for me the meaning of Jesus. Insofar as it was possible, I wanted to immerse myself in Jesus himself, to get as close as I could to seeing who he was—and that meant reading the Gospels, for that's where his life is described.[IV] So I turned to Matthew, Mark, Luke, and John, and I read and reread them (roughly a chapter a day) for fifteen years straight. After almost ten years of such reading, it finally dawned on me how often, in the first three Gospels, Jesus talked about the "kingdom of God." (I finally decided to count the references: 47 times in Matthew, 14 in Mark, 37 in Luke.)

In coming up out of this long, dark night of the soul, I found that my early, "conservative" image of God had crumbled. If "faith" could no longer rely on the literalness of biblical story, if God was not what literal belief in the Bible projected God to be, what was the point of being Christian? If God was not the image projected by belief in biblical literalism, how was I to get a better, deeper feel for who or what God is? What I found in the Gospels was an amazingly tough and alive Jesus, a man whose courage and bravery was so challenging it was actually frightening. He associated with the poor, with the peasant class, he taught and healed them, ate with them, walked everywhere he went, had no money, no home—*and* he was unrelentingly critical toward the educated, rich, and powerful—the civilized elite. He called them harsh and nasty names, and he refused to recant or back down. He made some people very, very angry. On the one hand, Jesus denounced the elite and utterly rejected their pious hypocrisy. On the other hand, he held out the notion of a "kingdom of God" as the way people could and should relate to one another. What did he intend by this "kingdom of God"?

When I finally got (or, at least, thought I got) the meaning of the "kingdom of God," this is what it was: Jesus' vision was to introduce a conduct of life among and between people that would, as spiritual yeast, leaven human consciousness, transform human behavior, and substitute a new organizing principle (the "kingdom of God") in place of the elite, top-down, aristocratic governing structure we call civilization. Jesus fully intended the kingdom of God, with its ethical underpinnings of radical servanthood and radical stewardship, to "yeast" away, dissolve, and digest the dominant principles of predatory civilization. The kingdom of God is a form of spiritual infection intending to alter our elemental human consciousness. The primary energy involved was bold, trusting, universal

---

IV. I realize biblical scholars say Paul's letters, or some of them, predate the Gospels. But that doesn't negate the fact that it's in the Gospels where the life and teaching of Jesus is described.

love. God, said Jesus, *is* this love. God is not "out there" somewhere, beyond the universe, watching life on Earth from a majestic, polished throne, benevolently (but also impatiently) detached. Don't expect this absent God to rescue you or support your righteous convictions.[V] If you *really* want to discover God, you are going to have to plunge into life beyond your comfort zone, risk everything you have, give away your wealth, renounce violence, and love so completely that you will even work at loving your enemies. And *then* a new, full, amazing understanding of God will come to you as you *do* these things—but a fuller image or richer revelation will *not* come if you refuse. You will, in fact, be stuck with your stage-scenery God as you stubbornly sit on your clean, moral hands.

So here, it seems, is a new place from which to consider the "conservative"/"liberal" divide. (Forgive me for always putting "liberal" and "conservative" in quotation marks, but the terms are very close to being descriptively worthless. "Conservatives" conserve nothing—unless, in principle, it's unborn babies—while "liberals" are steadily becoming more ecologically conservative.) "Conservatives" refuse to let go of a discredited image of God; and "liberals," wandering in the dark night of the soul, have yet to fully grasp the revolutionary, radical, life-transforming energy of the kingdom of God, especially as the kingdom of God is, as a spiritual concept with political consequences, the living inner core of democratic aspiration. "Liberals," in this sense, are like the Hebrews in the wilderness, in the Exodus story. Having escaped from the overbearing "conservative" Pharaoh, they are wandering in a state of reformulating confusion, needing to shed the tattered remnants of their "conservative" indoctrination before grasping a new and deeper revelation.

What's new in our time is that pharaonic civilization has become both global and universal. It used to be spotty, here and there, pockets of urban control in a world with lots of "wilderness" and noncivilized people and, of course, peasants—who were, in relation to the aristocracy, what cows or chickens are to a farmer. In those days, there might've been a civilized Egypt, run by a dictator Pharaoh, but there was still a lot of "wilderness" to escape to. Not any more. With Euro-American expansion from 1492 onward, the entire world has been subjected to rule by authoritarian

V. Albert Schweitzer, on page 57 of his 1933 book *Out of My Life and Thought*, essentially says that Jesus at first anticipated the "supernatural" imposition of the kingdom of God, quickly recognized his error, and thereafter completely settled on the kingdom's *ethical* unfolding.

urban power. This globalization never happened before in the history of the world.

What this means, I think, is that we are confronted with three major options as civilization conclusively demonstrates its unsustainability both culturally and ecologically. One option is that, with weapons of mass destruction, human beings will go even crazier and unleash enough of those weapons so that we'll all be dead. Extinct. All mammalian life could perish. A true End Times.

That's one option—and it is a totally possible option. The weapons are in place to make it happen.

Option two is that, as wealth once again congeals with greater and greater magnitude in the top one percent of the population (and that's what's happening both here and around the world), we will see a restoration of traditional aristocracy; and the rich, having *almost* lost political control because of an unanticipated upsurge in democratic energy, will see to it that they never lose control again. For the great bulk of us, life will be poor, hard, and brutal. We will have lost our opportunity to dissolve aristocracy and recreate society on the basis of democratic equality.

Option three is the one I'm hoping for. This one depends on our collective willingness to embrace the yeasty kingdom of God, on our willingness to love so fully that radical servanthood and radical stewardship, as principles of ethical behavior, become so convincingly strong that they spill out of their religious containers and begin to transform not only politics but the entire economy in the direction of libertarian, ecological, democratic socialism, the path the nineteenth-century Populists were on when they were defeated by Big Business.

My father, thank God, might've been a fundamentalist, but he was also a nineteenth-century character. He could never align himself with Big Business. In fact, I often thought he aggravated some of his SDA coreligionists by identifying the Lamb that becomes a Dragon, in the Book of Revelation, as the fate of America as it shed its democratic agrarian roots and became, instead, an industrial and military empire.

II

Having called my father a nineteenth-century character, I would like to take a moment to say why I've placed him in such time. This may seem silly because he was born on January 9, 1912, in Dawson, North Dakota, and he managed to live several years beyond the Y2K trolls.[VI] This timespan places my father almost entirely within the twentieth century. But I believe Henry was really a nineteenth-century man, and I think I can explain why that's so.

I've read enough American history to know that the period from 1885 until 1896 represents a great American turning point. That is, what changed in that decade was the primary economic and cultural basis of this country. Before the Civil War, the population was hugely rural and agrarian; but the Civil War (like World War II eighty years later) created huge changes in American society. During the Civil War, the North intensified war production by building factories and producing goods by means of mass production. The factory mode of production got an enormous war boost. An industrial/financial depression set in after the Civil War, in the 1870s, and farmers especially were driven into economic destitution because of low prices for agricultural commodities. But there were lots of farmers in those days and, in their desperation, they organized. One of their organizations was called the Farmers Alliance, created to build cooperatives by which farmers could achieve greater control over their economic circumstances. But the Farmers Alliance was always short of capital, short of money by which to build the infrastructure needed to make their cooperative effort work—grain storage facilities, for instance. Banks and private corporations tried to strangle the farmers' efforts. And so the farmers, realizing their situation needed not only an economic but also a political remedy, organized a political entity called the People's Party, otherwise known as the Populists. The Populists in the 1880s and on into the early 1890s elected lots of their own people to state legislatures, to many governorships, and quite a few people to Congress. They came fairly close to winning the U.S. presidential election of 1896. Close but no cigar.

With the election of 1896, the People's Party, built as it was on the psychologically strong but economically weak backs of impoverished farmers, began to collapse. They simply couldn't hold out any longer. Agrarian America—what we might call the Jeffersonian vision—was being defeated by the Hamiltonian octopus of banks and corporations, defeated at the polls by the power of money and industrialization arguing

VI. Henry died, at home, on August 26, 2009.

in behalf of "conservative," paternalistic authority. Even then, people were told, God hated radicals.

By 1920, urban population began to exceed rural population. And although the Great Depression of the 1930s seriously slowed industrial expansion and provided an unintentional opening for the growth of small-scale (and subsistence) farming, it was only a pause in the spread of industrialization and urbanization. And it was precisely in this Depression period of the 1930s when my father began to create his own small farm.

Not counting his early boyhood in the little prairie town of Dawson (where his parents were basically farmers, anyway), and the four months, more or less, he lived with his maternal grandparents in their big brick house in Merrill, Wisconsin, in 1921 and 1922, Henry was a totally rural person. Psychologically, his life was shaped not by the factories and cities of the twentieth century but by the farm mentality and countryside orientation of the nineteenth. His ideal, if we can call it that, was Jefferson's vision of small-scale farming.[VII] And, in that respect, my brothers (Bill and Joe) and I grew up in the thinning tail feathers of Jefferson's America. We got a glimpse, at least, of life with cookstoves, work horses, crosscut saws, huge gardens, scores of jars of home-canned vegetables and meat on racks in the cellar, and a one-room school, just down the gravel road, to which we could walk and be bored. We drank milk from the cows in the barn, dug potatoes in the garden, ate eggs from the chickens in the chicken house, and dragged lots of deer—legal and illegal—in from the woods. This was a life not yet fully intimidated by overarching corporate and political power, even as we kept an eye out for the game warden, a life still within the cultural stream of folk subsistence, ancient in its resources and roots, harkening back to our ethnic European peasant ancestors.

I haven't said much about what the People's Party stood for. It's been my experience that when I tell people what the Populists were about, a lot of them are shocked. The Populists, you see, developed a political program

VII. Ernest Becker, on page 291 of *The Structure of Evil*, makes a big distinction between democracy as an *ideal* versus democracy as an *ideology*. He embraces "ideal" and repudiates "ideology"—calling the latter a "wholly false definition of democracy as the freedom to buy and sell goods and to perpetuate the ideology of commerce." In broad principle I agree with Becker. But democracy as an "ideal" is, as a concept, much too rarified, abstract, and cerebral. It needs ecological and spiritual grounding in Creation. The radical stewardship and radical servanthood provisions of the kingdom of God provide exactly the required groundedness, especially when held in the warm embrace of indwelling Spirit.

that sought to control banks and corporations. The Populists were early socialists. A few of their policies came to fruition forty years later in the New Deal. Social Security, for instance, is at least in part due to the political energy of nineteenth-century Populists. Populists believed that mines and all forms of industrial infrastructure too big to be trusted in private hands—because such concentration tended toward aristocracy—were to be placed in the public domain. Railroads, for instance, were to be under public ownership and control. Private ownership was reserved for the small-scale. The large-scale was to be public. The diligent multiplicity of the democratically committed small-scale would see to it that the public large-scale was kept clean, efficient, and uncorrupted. That was what the nineteenth-century farmers believed in and struggled for—and also why bankers and industrialists fought them tooth and nail.[VIII]

My father was sufficiently removed from the 1880s to know practically nothing about the People's Party. But he always railed against the banks and corporations, against what he invariably called Big Business, and he was passionately for the health and survival of small farms. It was, I believe, a hard blow when the farm he and our mother made was sold out of the family in 1980, nearly fifty years after his first crop—of potatoes.

III

So why was the farm sold? Why didn't Bill or Joe or I take the farm over? The farm was, after all, if anything was, our father's life work, his biggest and most concentrated effort, his creation. He made a small, diversified dairy farm out of 120 acres of brush, stumps, rocks, swamps, scrub trees, and soil burned by forest fires. It was an effort we might even call heroic. And I mean that seriously.

We brothers failed to take over the farm for a variety of reasons. First, if our father was a nineteenth-century peasant, we brothers were twentieth-century school kids whose indoctrinated upbringing was being shaped by electricity, radio, television, tractors, milking machines, store-bought goods, years of compulsory education, and a pervasive commercialization of our minds. All this lured and beckoned us from the backwardness of

VIII. For a list of the political planks in the Populist platform, see page 137 in Richard Stiller's *Queen of Populists: The Story of Mary Elizabeth Lease*. The Populist planks included reform of national currency and a graduated income tax, postal savings banks, an eight-hour day for industrial workers, direct election of U.S. senators, and government ownership of railroads, telephone, and telegraph.

farming and on into the forward progress of the city. Second, our parents also aspired to commercial success. Our father worked mightily to make his little homestead into a small business, and, by so doing, he let go of many subsistence and sustainable practices in favor of growth, money, and machines. He abandoned his little log house. He built a barn too big for the land he owned, and he overburdened the land with more cattle than it could carry. He quit smoking his own meat and didn't have much patience for gardening. He quit work horses for tractors, a hay loader for a baler, felt a privately owned junky combine was better than cooperative threshing, and, although he was clerk of the town school board for many years, he never developed or embraced an educational philosophy that would've included community life or the natural world in what was to be taught or learned in the one-room schools. His educational views, like his religious views, were entirely conventional. If you got a lickin' at school, you should get one as well when you got home. Learning to "mind" was a high priority, another requisite form of obedience.[IX]

Our mother, I think, had a quicker, more probing intelligence, but she too strove for lifestyle improvement. Her guides were the mass-circulation women's magazines of the 1950s—*Redbook* and *Ladies Home Journal*—with their glossy photographs of houses, interiors, and appliances that showed what *real* living was supposed to be. Bill and I were, in her desires, to be a doctor and a clergyman (although I can't seem to remember who was to be which); but Joe escaped those expectations when our mother's cancer—which I suspect to this day may have been caused by the DDT we used as fly spray in the barn—put her on a terrible slide toward an early death. She died before she was fifty, in February of 1963.

In my estimation, we brothers left the farm because farming as a way of life requires sustained self-provisioning practices, and all of us—we brothers *and* our parents—were moving psychologically in a direction that rejected subsistence skills and homestead life. In other words, we were all caught in the flow toward relative affluence and indeterminate

IX. In some ways, school was *the* institution that channeled social life in a utopian direction. That's not to minimize the role of the church, for instance, in the maintenance of transcendent power and the promotion of deference to such power. But school provided the day-to-day compulsory boredom, the sheer impoundment of youthful physicality, the systematic quarantine from nature, and the pervasive indoctrination in utopian progress by which democratic eutopianism was strangled in its crib. When, later, I read Paul Goodman's *Compulsory Miseducation*, I was stunned that an educated man could see the problem with such clarity and honesty.

progress. We did not have any built-in cultural or spiritual resistances (such as the Amish have) to that flow. Everything whispered "Progress!" even if "progress" was killing our mother with its "better living through chemistry." Commercial farming without the life satisfactions of self-provisioning is only another kind of business, and is to be considered only through the lens of abstract monetary calculation. For us, it was too much work for too little pay. So we left.

Now it can also be asserted that we left for other reasons, including a pervasive psychological bleakness, a lack of conviviality and intimacy. I think that's true. That is, there was bleakness, particularly with our mother's protracted illness and death. But I also believe that the psychological bleakness was largely a product, directly and indirectly, of a deeper but more elusive cultural bleakness that was the inevitable consequence of abandoning both subsistence and cooperative practices. Cooperative *culture* was disintegrating; both neighborhood and family life were becoming unglued. "Progress" made people restless, envious, bitter, and unhappy, no longer content with "homemade" or "enough." Abandoning subsistence and cooperative practices also made us increasingly incompetent in the skills and aptitudes of self-provisioning, so we simply had to turn toward the abstractions of Progress in order to feel we were "getting somewhere."

People in truly subsistence cultures are rarely bored. Their lives are too complex for boredom. They have too much freedom or at least too much practical competence. They know how to do too many things. They are not *trained* in boredom or conditioned to live in a state of boredom the way we were trained in school, in the factory, in work measured by time and money. People raised in truly subsistence cultures have a sense of belonging, of work and leisure far different than our time-equals-money orientation. To be modern is to be restless and bored, and we were feeding rather lavishly at the trough of restless (and even reckless) boredom. "Progress" was our drug, and we could never get enough of it.

IV

I remember being puzzled for years why my father could get so enthused about the books of Daniel and Revelation but, as a self-professed Christian, hardly ever talk about Jesus, and basically never talk about the social significance of the Gospels. It took me a long time to realize that for my father the kingdom of God, mentioned so many times in the first three Gospels, was not a concept he really knew how to talk about. Why could he talk so vehemently about End Times and so little, if at all, about the kingdom of God? Why? Which of those—preoccupations, perhaps—is more basic to Christian conviction? Is it that "radical" Christians turn to the kingdom of God for guidance and understanding while "conservative" Christians turn to apocalyptic projections? I think we're back, at least in part, to questions regarding myth and biblical literalism versus metaphorical or ethical explication. Perhaps I can illustrate the point somewhat whimsically by means of a three-part logical device called a syllogism. Here are the steps: #1: Eternity is all-embracing time. #2: We are living in time. #3: Therefore we are living in eternity.

The mentality that accompanies a truly subsistence life, a truly subsistent and sustainable culture, lives largely within the leisure of eternity. The mentality that breaks out of subsistence life and enters the empire of Progress lives in a calculation that equates time with money, separates itself from eternity, and no longer trusts that sufficiency is adequate. It *seizes* control, strives to coerce nature (or, perhaps, a peasantry) into greater and greater productivity, and, in so doing, creates a reservoir of perpetual anxiety the "cure" for which is even greater levels of control and coercion. In my estimation, the imposition of aristocratic civilization five or six thousand years ago—and by "imposition" I mean that an armed and deadly aristocracy expropriated as much as possible from the peasants and forced those peasants to work excessively hard for a bare survival—these civilized aristocrats began to create the mental/social condition that today is called "alienation." At the upper level it created a sense of predatory, luxurious entitlement, and at the lower level a perpetual anxiety based on fear of authority and enforced scarcity. Civilization created institutionalized alienation, enforced its perpetuation, and made it "normal." Alienation among the oppressed is a state of mind that also yearns for relief and release.

My first exposure to the factory, in the summer of 1964, just after graduating from high school, taught me how deeply the men *hated* their jobs, for at the end of the day they punched their timecards furiously fast and *ran* across the parking lot to their cars before speeding away in a cloud of dust. Farm work (like picking stones) could be hard and boring, but it was never *that* boring. Factory boredom was never "normal" on the farm.

So if life under conditions of civilization creates epidemic alienation, an alienation that metastasizes as civilization reaches global proportions, as the base is taken up into the superstructure, then part of the mental energy within apocalyptic religions is the creating of expectations that anticipate release and relief. Christ is coming! God is going to smash something flat! We are going to be liberated from our mental anguish!

I don't think people in noncivilized subsistence cultures need these apocalyptic fantasies. Such people are not living lives of constant, endemic, epidemic alienation. They have their feet, as it were, in the functional leisure of eternity.

Here, I believe, is the connection to the key concept of Jesus in the first three Gospels. Jesus repeatedly talked about the kingdom of God being "at hand," as he also called us to repent of our selfish ways—that is, to let go of those selfish ways, to give them up, to quit clinging to them. The Lord's Prayer explicitly has us ask for that "kingdom" to come "on Earth as it is in heaven" (Luke 11:2–4). We're supposed to *want* it and *ask* for it. The kingdom of God, rooted in the ethical principles of radical servanthood and radical stewardship, is a richer, fuller, higher, and deeper kind of subsistence life and cooperative culture, a life no longer seriously constrained by tribal, ethnic, racial, or gender boundary, no longer fenced in by chronic anxiety. It is life in eternity raised to a universal level of consciousness and determined to "yeast" the entire conduct of life, including civilized institutions, into wholesome, democratic subsistence. (This is, I think, the hidden, prophetic energy within Green politics.)

And so, it seems, biblical literalists for the most part are overwhelmingly alienated people, people who are so used to alienation as normative that their idea of ultimate relief is to see the entire world get smashed or blown to Hell. This is why, in the really big and scary picture, many fundamentalist Christians can hardly wait for even bloodier war to erupt in the Middle East: because Armageddon brings the Second Coming of Christ, because Armageddon ushers in *relief*. But all this (aside from its political reality as self-fulfilling "prophecy") is a deadly, morbid, and even sadistic fantasy created by taking symbolic language literally, by refusing to look real history in the eyes, and by scorning the kingdom of God as impossible on Earth. That scorning is the great sin of fundamentalism. It has taken civilized alienation to a new level by giving it apocalyptic sanction. And if the Age of the Holy Ghost really is the Age of the Daughter, this may be the sin that will not and cannot be forgiven because for sin to be forgiven it must also be repented and let go of. (The kingdom of God is *not* a theocracy, either, such as is imagined by the most politically hard-line of the Christian Right. Theocracy is biblical literalism merged with civilizational governing structures. Theocracy is not the realization or the fulfillment of the kingdom of God, but is its spiritual opposite. Theocracy is what happens when spirituality says yes to the Devil, as can be inferred from Matthew 4 and Luke 4.)

Jesus taught over and over that the way into eternity was to follow his footsteps, and that means in part to renounce violence and fantasies of revenge and retaliation, of "lording it over." To live in this eternity means to *love* God, *love* your neighbor, and even *love* your enemy. If Jesus is, as Paul the Apostle says, the "perfect image" of God, then God is a nonviolent, suffering servant who is patiently waiting for us to catch on. In the Gospels, there is no murdering sword in the mouth of Jesus, only healing and forgiveness, only servanthood and stewardship, only subsistence, sufficiency, and sustainability—and sharp anger (conveyed with words and not a sword) directed toward those who wrap themselves in the flags of church and state, who worship a theatrical cartoon God, who live fearfully and protectively inside their bubble of anxious alienation.

V

So far as I know, no economist disputes the fact that it was the Second World War, with its virtually unlimited federal spending for war materials, that lifted the United States out of the Great Depression. And it seems that many economists recognize that the commercial prosperity in the United States since the end of World War II was due to the federal maintenance of a permanent war economy—although it seems the burst housing bubble is indicative of an irreversible downward slide. [X] Our underlying fear (probably more subconscious than conscious) is that a serious pruning of the Pentagon budget would plunge us right back to 1940, right back

---

X. Lewis Mumford on page 225 of *The Pentagon of Power*, talks about "The impossibility of maintaining a high level of productivity without a more equitable distribution of both income and goods," and that the "only alternative to this in terms of the current power ideology [is] either 'pyramid building' or preparations for war." But we seem to be reaching the end of the war-spending options simultaneously with the collapse of utopian consumerism. The ecological crisis demands a vastly reduced consumption—radical stewardship. Our true ethical heritage requires socialist sharing—radical servanthood.

into an industrial depression that nobody (short of war spenders) knows how to suspend.

We know from a century and a half of experience that the capitalist economy, controlled by bankers and corporations, moves steadily towards a maximized constriction of small-scale farming and a maximized expansion of financialized golden parachutes. The demographics of both farming and financial institutions speak, as it were, for themselves.[XI] From this knowledge, and from a deepened understanding not only of ecological tolerances (which subject is always obliquely in the news these days), but also as our minds slowly are transformed from literal Bible worship to an embrace of the kingdom of God, we can begin to grasp a Green political order of libertarian, democratic, ecological socialism, in which a public *industry* of durable goods gets folded into a cooperative *culture* of shops, local services, small schools, small-scale farming, and gardening.

So my father's impulse to identify Big Business as the negative, controlling force in both the economy and in politics was and is essentially correct. In his lifetime, born less than twenty years after the Populists were defeated, he was still in the stream of the Jeffersonian vision as it continued to play itself out, as the formal cash economy infiltrated into virtually every nook and cranny of private, domestic life (think Wal-Mart and internet spam). Globalization, with its cultural and ecological "blowback," is forcing us all to choose between rival governing principles: either civilization, which is bringing us speedily to global disaster, or the Green

---

XI. Although I am too far removed from the inner workings of the financial system to know how close to economic collapse we actually were in the fall of 2008 (or what the consequences of such a collapse might have been), it is obvious since the crisis that neither the systemic flaws nor the human manipulators of those flaws have been removed. While I am inclined to be sympathetic toward bold proposals coming from the Left—like Robert Pollin's "18 Million Jobs by 2012: How Obama Can Save His Presidency," in the March 8, 2010, issue of *The Nation*—such proposals are typically devoid of agricultural analysis, including the extent to which the industrialization of agriculture has massively reduced agricultural employments and thereby lifted the entire economy out onto the brittle utopian twigs of a capitalist system that is not only dangerously top-heavy but has ungrounded the entire human economy from its folk roots. Yet for all the economistic esotery—derivative swaps and all the rest—our basic human need for food, clothing, and shelter has not moved one iota from our ancient past (although that truth has been conceptually buried in the utopian landfill of plastic abstractions). What's needed is folk restoration of food, clothing, and shelter. The growth of a Green, utopian economy requires such restoration, and the health and vitality of a Green, utopian culture is proportionate to the depth and magnitude of a Green, utopian economy. Thus will folk cultural evolution be resurrected from its brutal burial in the bleak dungeons of utopian civility.

kingdom of God, which offers us an immense reconciliation embracing everything from the economic to the spiritual. That the outcome remains in doubt, that people can't figure out which choice to make, is proof of how deeply civilized mythology is embedded in our minds, along with its hysterical and erratic companion—religious fundamentalism.

VI

Finally, I want to say a pleading word about science to those who are biblical literalists. I believe we have to attend to the investigations of science, and we have to take those conclusions seriously. That's not to say that science ever arrives at some final truth, or that everything "science" says is absolutely or unconditionally true. But we are foolish in the extreme to blow off what science has discovered, as if such discoveries were of no consequence or epistemologically optional. The fundamentalist rejection of science is based overwhelmingly on the desire of fundamentalists to protect their literalistic image of God—as if God needed protection. The *emotion* under all this seems to be fear—fear of a very harsh, demanding God who will, in the end, throw almost everybody into Hell, saving only the most obedient few for an eternity of bliss.

If science has undermined our traditional image of God, we are bound to search for more appropriate and intimate images. The famous German theologian Paul Tillich called God the "Ground of Being." That's a thought very much worth pondering. And I have toyed with the concept of "village" of God rather than "kingdom" of God. But the most recent notion that's come to mind (a purely peasant thought, no doubt) is—God is in a way like dirt, like soil, like humus, or like compost. I say this because soil is the product of death and decay, excrement, dead leaves, grass clippings, vegetable waste, cow bones, deer poop, bird feathers, and gopher pee—all of it composted with minerals, sunshine, and rainwater into this rich, wonderful substance that gardeners love—compost. What's alive eventually returns to compost. Ashes to ashes, dust to dust. That this is true on the material plane is obvious and requires no explanation. It is the vital stuff out of which new life grows.

But what happens to our *spiritual* energy? It's here I begin to imagine God as a spiritually digestive compost bin, the place or dimension where our *spiritual* energy goes to or resides when we die. If this seems theologically crude (to put it mildly), it probably is. But it has the advantage of conceptually greenhousing our spirituality. We are not, in this organic economy, shipping our spiritual capital off to China in exchange for the heavenly trinkets supplied by a divine Wal-Mart, nor riding in a fancy casket inside a cement box, well-dressed and flush with funeral parlor rouge, on our way to a distant, otherworldly heaven, just parked temporarily, you know, six feet under, waiting for the divine UPS or Federal Express truck to honk its horn. If we are to have a life after death, it's God's job to provide that life, not yours or mine. In other words, quit worrying about what's going to happen after you're dead. That's out of our control. Stop pretending—or imagining—that it's not.

If you want to *love* God (as opposed to fearing death or scheming how to save your precious mortal bacon), then your job, like mine, is to love your neighbor as you love yourself, even the neighbor who is your enemy. Your job, like mine, is to put aside notions of retaliation, revenge, and retribution, and embrace the radical servanthood and radical stewardship contained within the kingdom of God. As Jesus says in Luke 7:47, "It is the man who is forgiven little who shows little love." For those in control, however, it is stubborn and even arrogant pride that refuses to repent; and where there is little repentance there is also little forgiveness and therefore, sorrowfully, little love. As Barbara Tuchman puts it, "Rigidifying leads to increase of investment and the need to protect egos; policy founded upon error multiplies, never retreats."[1]

Science helps teach us what God is not; and for that, despite the pain as our illusions get wrecked, we should be grateful. Getting to a fuller understanding of God simply has to be a good and growing thing, even if it hurts. Entering and practicing the kingdom of God is how we begin to learn anew what God may be. Those who prefer to stand on the outside, merely looking in, have nothing useful to contribute, even as they may stride the stage, wave Bibles in the air, and shout about salvation. Hot air comes in a variety of interesting, pressurized containers.

To some extent, I wish to beg your pardon. I've been long-winded and a hog of your time. But this has been my opportunity to respond to my father as fully as I've been able, at least in this fairly short way. I was, perhaps, his most regular companion over the last twenty-five years of his life. He helped build the log house my wife Susanna and I are eager to return to. And we—Susanna and I—tried to be present for my step-mother Viola, who died in 2004, and for Henry, in their last years and days.

I am not worried in the least about my father's "salvation." In Matthew 25, the conditions for salvation are specifically spelled out—feed the hungry, provide water to the thirsty, entertain the stranger, clothe the naked, tend the sick, visit the prisoner. My father, tightwad that he was, helped other people survive from the time he was a child. He provided for his large family while still a teenager, took in his maternal grandparents when he was only twenty-one, was our mother's nurse as she lay dying, housed a temperamental, paraplegic step-son for twenty-five years, raised two step-grandchildren as if they were his own, took daily care of his second wife as she drifted into senility—and performed many other acts of mercy, compassion, and sheer generosity known and unknown. If there is life after death, I presume God will wave him in; and, unless he stops to argue with God about what the Bible *really* says about salvation, he may just go in dancing.

But *our* job, the job of the living, is right here on Earth. As Thoreau apparently said on his deathbed, "One world at a time."[2] Anybody who tells you it's not one world at a time is living in an escapist fantasy; and the big problem with escapist fantasies is how awesomely selfish and violent those fantasies can become, how they grow and become deadly—like those of the Christian Right today, slouching toward Armageddon to be "born" in a ball of fire. Humble, earthly love is the only way out of this globalized mess we civilized humans have created. All else is toxic hot air, some of it potentially lethal.

NOTES

1. Tuchman, *March*, 383.
2. Thoreau, *Faith*, 17.

Bibliography

Adams, Brooks. *The Law of Civilization and Decay*. New York: Vintage, 1955.

Allan, Tony. *Prophecies: 4,000 Years of Prophets, Visionaries and Predictions*. New York: Barnes & Noble, 2006.

Anderson, Perry. "Made in USA." In *The Nation*, April 2, 2007.

Augustine. *The City of God*. New York: Random House, 1950.

Bachevich, Andrew. "The Semiwarriors." In *The Nation*, April 23, 2007.

Bachofen, Johann Jakob. *Myth, Religion, and Mother Right: Selected Writings of J. J. Bachofen*. Translated by Ralph Manheim. Princeton, NJ: Princeton University Press, 1992.

Bailie, Gil. *Violence Unveiled: Humanity at the Crossroads*. New York: Crossroad, 1995.

Beard, Charles A. "Introduction." In *The Law of Civilization and Decay*. New York: Vintage, 1955.

Becker, Ernest. *The Structure of Evil: An Essay on the Unification of the Science of Men*. New York: Braziller, 1968.

Birkel, Michael. *A Near Sympathy: The Timeless Quaker Wisdom of John Woolman*. Richmond, IN: Friends United, 2003.

Borg, Marcus. *The Heart of Christianity*. San Francisco: Harper San Francisco, 2003.

Bowe, John. *Nobodies: Modern American Slave Labor and the Dark Side of the New Global Economy*. New York: Random House, 2007.

Branch, Taylor. *Parting the Waters: America in the King Years 1954–63*. New York: Simon and Schuster, 1988.

Brown, Norman O. *Life Against Death: The Psychoanalytical Meaning of History*. Middletown, CT: Wesleyan University Press, 1959.

———. *Love's Body*. New York: Vintage, 1966.

Callahan, Daniel. *The Tyranny of Survival*. New York: Macmillan, 1975.

Campbell, Joseph. *Myths to Live By*. New York: Bantam, 1988.

Carroll, James. *House of War: The Pentagon and the Disastrous Rise of American Power*. Boston: Houghton Mifflin, 2006.

Cayley, David. *The Rivers North of the Future: The Testament of Ivan Illich*. Toronto: House of Anansi, 2005.

Chomsky, Noam. *The New Military Humanism: Lessons from Kosovo*. Monroe, ME: Common Courage, 1999.

Cobb, John B., Jr. "Spiritual Paradigms of the Western World and Non-Western Alternatives." In *Theology and Corporate Conscience: Essays in Honor of Frederick Herzog*, edited by Douglas Meeks, Jurgen Moltmann, and Frederick R. Trost. Minneapolis: Kirk House, 1999.

Commager, Henry Steele. *The American Mind*. New Haven: Yale University Press, 1950.

Crossan, John Dominic. *God and Empire: Jesus against Rome, Then and Now*. New York: Harper Collins, 2007.

de Riencourt, Amaury. *The Coming Caesars*. New York: Coward-McCann, 1957.

Diamond, Jarad. *Collapse: How Societies Choose to Fail or Succeed*. New York: Viking, 2005.

Diwan, Romesh and Mark Lutz. "Introduction." In *Essays in Gandhian Economies*. New York: Intermediate Technology Development Group of North America, 1987.

Dupuy, Jean-Pierre. "Detour and Sacrifice." In *The Challenges of Ivan Illich*. Albany: State University of New York Press, 2002.

Ellsberg, Daniel. *Secrets: A Memoir of Vietnam and the Pentagon Papers*. New York: Viking, 2002.

Esteva, Gustavo. *Celebration of Zapatismo*. Oaxaca, Mexico: Ediciones Basta, 2006.

Frank, Thomas. *What's the Matter with Kansas?* New York: Metropolitan, 2004.

Fraser, Steve. "Take the Money and Run." In *The Nation*, April 2, 2007.

Gilk, Paul. *Green Politics Is Eutopian*. Eugene, OR: Wipf & Stock, 2008.

———. *Nature's Unruly Mob: Farming and the Crisis in Rural Culture*. Eugene, OR: Wipf & Stock, 2009.

Gish, Arthur G. *Hebron Journal: Stories of Nonviolent Peacemaking*. Scottsdale, PA: Herald Press, 2001.

Gonzalez, Justo L. *The Story of Christianity: The Reformation to the Present Day*. New York: Harper Collins, 1985.

Goodman, Paul. *Compulsory Miseducation*. New York: Horizon, 1964.

Goodwyn, Lawrence. *The Populist Moment: A Short History of the Agrarian Revolt*. New York: Oxford University Press, 1978.

Haldeman, H. R. *The Haldeman Diaries: Inside the Nixon Whitehouse*. New York: G. P. Putnam's, 1994.

Harrington, Michael. *Socialism*. New York: Saturday Review, 1970.

Hedges, Chris. *American Fascists: The Christian Right and the War on America*. New York: Free Press, 2006.

———. "Hands Off Iran." In *The Nation*, December 10, 2007.

Heschel, Abraham J. *The Prophets*. New York: Harper Touchbooks, 1969.

Hobsbawm, E. J. *Industry and Empire*. Baltimore: Penguin, 1976.

Hoinacki, Lee, and Carl Mitcham, editors. *The Challenges of Ivan Illich*. Albany: State University of New York Press, 2002.

Illich, Ivan. "The Cultivation of Conspiracy." In *The Challenges of Ivan Illich*. Albany: State University of New York Press, 2002.

Jones, Seth G. *In the Graveyard of Empires: America's War in Afghanistan*. New York: Norton, 2009.

Judis, John B. "Death Grip." In *The New Republic*, August 27, 2007.

Kast, David. "Hard Times." Academic paper prepared for "Politics, Pluralism, and Religion," a conference sponsored by Society of Indian Philosophy and Religion at Minnesota State University, Mankato, Minnesota, April 13–14, 2007.

Kaufman, Maynard. *Adapting to the End of Oil: Toward an Earth-Centered Spirituality*. Xlibris, 2008.

Klein, Naomi. "A Trial for Thousands Denied Trial." In *The Nation*, March 12, 2007.

———. "Disaster Capitalism." In *Harper's*, October 2007.

Kunstler, James Howard. *The Long Emergency: Surviving the Converging Crises of the Twenty-first Century*. New York: Atlantic Monthly, 2005.

Kurlansky, Mark. *1968: The Year That Rocked the World*. New York: Random House, 2005.

Lakoff, George. *Don't Think of an Elephant!* White River Junction, VT: Chelsea Green, 2004.

Lewis, C. S. *The Last Battle*. New York: Collier, 1970.

Lings, Martin. "Saint Malachy's Prophecy." In *Parabola*, Spring 1996.

McGovern, Arthur. *Marxism: An American Christian Perspective*. Maryknoll, NY: Orbis, 1980.

Merton, Thomas. "Introduction." In *The City of God*. New York: Random House, 1950.

———. *The Silent Life*. New York: Dell, 1959.

Mosse, George L. *Toward the Final Solution: A History of European Racism*. New York: Harper & Row, 1978.

Mumford, Lewis. *The Myth of the Machine*. New York: Harcourt, Brace & World, 1966.

———. *The Pentagon of Power*. New York: Harcourt, Brace & Jovanovich, 1970.

———. "Utopia, the City, and the Machine." In *Interpretations and Forecasts: 1922–1972*. New York: Harcourt, Brace & Jovanovich, 1979.

Myers, Ched. *Binding the Strong Man: A Political Reading of Mark's Story of Jesus*. Maryknoll, NY: Orbis, 2008.

Norberg-Hodge, Helena. *Ancient Futures: Learning from Ladakh*. San Francisco: Sierra Club, 1992.

Pagels, Elaine. *Beyond Belief: The Secret Gospel of Thomas*. New York: Random House, 2005.

———. *The Gnostic Gospels*. New York: Random House, 1979.

Parenti, Christian. "Empire Fall." In *The Nation*, March 12, 2007.

Phillips, Kevin. *Bad Money: Reckless Finance, Failed Politics, and the Global Crisis of American Capitalism*. New York: Viking, 2008.

———. *Boiling Point: Democrats, Republicans, and the Decline of Middle-Class Prosperity*. New York: Random House, 1993.

Polanyi, Karl. *The Great Transformation*. Boston: Beacon, 1957.

Pollin, Robert. "18 Million Jobs by 2012: How Obama Can Save His Presidency." In *The Nation*, March 8, 2010.

Postman, Neil. *Technopoly: The Surrender of Culture to Technology*. New York: Vintage, 1993.

Robinson, Dave. "The Perfect Storm." In *The Catholic Peace Voice*, Fall 2007.

Sachs, Wolfgang. "One World." In *The Development Dictionary: A Guide to Knowledge as Power*. New York: Palgrave, 2003.

Said, Edward. *Culture and Imperialism*. New York: Vintage, 1993.

Sale, Kirkpatrick. *After Eden: The Evolution of Human Domination*. Durham, NC: Duke University Press, 2006.

Schell, Jonathan. "The Fifty-Year War." In *The Nation*, November 30, 2009.

———. "Understanding Massachusetts." In *The Nation*, February 15, 2010.

Schweitzer, Albert. *Out of My Life and Thought*. New York: Henry Holt and Company, 1955.

Slattery, W. Michael. *Jesus the Warrior? Historical Christian Perspectives and Problems on the Morality of War and the Waging of Peace*. Milwaukee: Marquette University Press, 2007.

Smith, Henry Nash. *Virgin Land*. New York: Vintage, 1950.

Soelle, Dorothee. *Against the Wind: Memoir of a Radical Christian*. Translated by Barbara and Martin Rumscheidt. Minneapolis: Fortress, 1999.

Bibliography

Spengler, Oswald. *The Decline of the West*. An abridged edition by Helmut Werner, prepared by Arthur Helps, translated by Charles Francis Atkinson. New York: Alfred A. Knopf, 1962.

Stiller, Richard. *Queen of Populists: The Story of Mary Elizabeth Lease*. New York: Dell, 1976.

Strange, Marty. *Family Farming: A New Economic Vision*. Lincoln, NE: University of Nebraska Press, 2008.

Stringfellow, William. "The Constantinian Status Quo." In *A Keeper of the Word: Selected Writings of William Stringfellow*, edited by Bill Wylie Kellerman. Grand Rapids, MI: Eerdmans, 1994.

Swedish, Margaret. *Living Beyond the "End of the World."* Maryknoll, NY: Orbis, 2008.

Tawney, R. H. *The Acquisitive Society*. New York: Harcourt, Brace & World, 1948.

Thoreau, Henry David. *Faith in a Seed: The Dispersion of Seeds and Other Late Natural History Writings*, edited by Bradley P. Dean. Washington, DC: Island, 1995.

———. "On the Duty of Civil Disobedience." In *Walden*. New York: Holt, Rinehart and Winston, [no date].

Tillich, Paul. *On the Boundary*. New York: Scribner's, 1966.

Toynbee, Arnold J. *Civilization on Trial*. New York: Oxford University Press, 1948.

Tuchman, Barbara W. *The March of Folly: From Troy to Vietnam*. New York: Alfred A. Knopf, 1984.

Zinn, Howard. *A People's History of the United States: 1492-Present*. New York: Harper-Collins, 1999.